Tales from the Syracuse Hardwood

Bud Poliquin

Sports Publishing L.L.C.
www.SportsPublishingLLC.com

Director of production: Susan M. Moyer
Project manager: Greg Hickman
Developmental editor: Doug Hoepker
Copy editors: Cynthia L. McNew and Holly Birch
Dust jacket design: Kenny O'Brien

ISBN: 1-58261-735-x

Printed in the United States.

SPORTS PUBLISHING L.L.C.
www.SportsPublishingLLC.com

It's been said that writer's block is that affliction which attacks some authors between the ears, a malady I have often suffered. But thanks to the folks who opened their mental vaults to me in the couple of months following the Orangemen's triumph in the 2003 national title game, such was not the case on this project.

Tales from the Syracuse Hardwood, *then, is dedicated to those who shared and to the Syracuse University basketball fans whose passion has made the memories even more valuable.*

It is also dedicated to my bride, Kathleen, and to our two kids, Nathan and Caitlin, each of whom now knows what I was doing in the basement all those nights.

Acknowledgments

A special thanks to the following who were kind enough to share their thoughts and/or memories with me.

Dick Ableman, Rafael Addison, Carmelo Anthony, Mary Anthony, Mike Barlow, Murray Bernthal, Mel Besdin, Frank Beyer, Jim Boeheim, Roosevelt Bouie, Manny Breland, Jim Brown, Lou Carnesecca, Perez Celis, Billy Celuck, Lou Cinquino, Jason Cipolla, Vinnie Cohen, Roy Danforth, Rick Dean, Sherman Douglas, Kueth Duany, Dennis DuVal, Leo Eisner, Billy Gabor, Bob Gilbert, Allen Griffin, Joe Hamelin, Vaughn Harper, Herman Harried, Jason Hart, George Hicker, Tim Higgins, Mike Hopkins, Larry Kimball, Kevin King, Manny Klutchkowski, Bob Kouwe, Jimmy Lee, Mike Lee, Donovan McNabb, Lawrence Moten, Royce Newell, Louis Orr, Ken Osier, Sam Penceal, Leo Rautins, Chuck Richards, Dolph Schayes, Earnie Seibert, Dale Shackleford, Owen Shapiro, Steve Shaw, Lazarus Sims, Bill Smith, Howard Triche, Carl Vernick, Dwayne "Pearl" Washington and Mark Ziolko.

Additionally, I salute the following:

1) Leo Eisner, the long-time member of the Syracuse University Hardwood Club; Larry Kimball, SU's Sports Information Director Emeritus; and Kathleen Poliquin, my bride, for their dedicated editing;

2) Pete Moore of SU's Department of Communications, for his invaluable research assistance;

3) Frank Ordonez, for his unsurpassed expertise with a camera;

4) Molly Elliott of the *Syracuse Post-Standard*, for her keen eye for photography and cheery grit; and

5) The *Syracuse Post-Standard* newspaper, for allowing the generous and unfettered use of its library resources.

Contents

Foreword

Whenever I think about how close I came to never attending Syracuse University and never becoming an Orangeman, I shudder.

I started my college basketball career at the University of Minnesota, and then actually transferred to Marshall University, before finally landing at SU in the fall of 1979. I ended up spending three seasons as an Orangeman—four, counting my redshirt year—and left school as a proud graduate in 1983. And when I did, I took a lot of wonderful memories with me.

There was, of course, the famous triple-overtime conquest of Villanova in the 1981 Big East Conference championship game—which is discussed in some detail on the pages of this book—followed by the controversial "snub" by the NCAA Tournament selection committee that inspired our run to the finals of the NIT in New York City.

And there were our 11 victories over our fiercest Big East rivals—Georgetown, St. John's, Connecticut and Villanova. And there was our trip, short though it may have been, to the 1983 NCAA Tournament during my senior year.

But beyond all of that were the great times I had with my teammates.

You know, during my "cup of coffee" in the NBA, my teammates included the likes of Julius "Dr. J" Erving, Bobby Jones, Moses Malone, Mo Cheeks, Dominique Wilkins, Doc Rivers, Tree Rollins and even that one-time nemesis from Georgetown, Patrick Ewing. I cherish the lessons learned and the time spent with them

But at SU, I played with Roosevelt Bouie, Louis Orr, Dale Shackleford, Danny Schayes and Rafael Addison, just to name a few—and I'm equally proud of that. As they are all brought to life in the pages that follow, you'll see why.

That's why I'm so happy to provide this opening tip for *Tales from the Syracuse Hardwood.* I've got to tell you that I've always liked Bud Poliquin, if only because his son—a baseball player, but I've forgiven him for that—used to babysit for my kids. But I like him a little more now that this book has gone to print. See, I thought I knew a fair amount about my Orangemen, and I believed I'd heard most of the stories—even the ones about my pals. But Bud proved me wrong.

Calvin Murphy's 68-point game against us in 1968? The sure-fire bet that Roy Danforth always wins out on Cape Cod? Jim Boeheim, my old coach, as a golf coach? Jim Brown, the basketball player? Doves flying around Manley Field House? Papa Schayes punching out an eight-foot rabbit? It's all in here. And more.

Why, as hinted above, there's even a story about a curly-haired Canadian kid who ended the longest—and maybe, the best— game ever played in the Carrier Dome…and did so with something other than basketball on his mind. Yep, that would be me. And I doubt I'll ever forget it.

But enough. There are tales to be read and then told to friends. Bud Poliquin has done the reporting and the writing. It's your turn now to do the enjoying.

Leo Rautins, proud Orangeman, Class of 1983
July 2003

Introduction

The hat gave him away. The big loony hat that might well have been worn down Bourbon Street by any visiting linoleum salesman at the Mardi Gras. Jim Boeheim, normally as cheery as a blister, walked off the airplane from New Orleans looking blissfully silly beneath the very odd lid…and everybody knew. They just knew.

Things were different in Syracuse. Things were better, brighter, bouncier. And if the nutty hat atop Boeheim's head hadn't provided enough of a clue, there was, for further evidence, the national championship trophy he was lugging through Hancock International Airport.

The Syracuse University Orangemen had done it. They'd won the 2003 title by surviving the Final Four at the Louisiana Superdome, bashing Texas and outlasting Kansas before nearly 110,000 fans. They were the best college basketball team in all the land. And suddenly, it was as if color—reds and purples, blues and yellows, greens and pinks—had sprouted in Pleasantville.

"I came here in 1962," said Boeheim, the SU coach who has become the sunrise and sunset of Orange basketball. "And when I got here, the people were still pretty high on the championship the football team had won in 1959. And that was more than 40 years ago when sports didn't have the same magnitude. So, I think there's going to be some life to this thing."

It was amazing. The Orangemen had played basketball since 1901 and in the middle of their run, in 1955, the old Syracuse Nationals had captured the NBA championship. So, Central and Upstate New York had long embraced the game that predated even Vic Hanson, cruised along through Danny Schayes and glowed beneath Carmelo Anthony's wide smile.

But this—this was a revelation, even to Boeheim, who was overwhelmed upon his return from New Orleans.

"I think I've finally figured it out," he said. "Normally, 40 to 50 percent of the people around Syracuse follow our program. Or whatever the percentage is. Maybe it's 60 percent. I don't know. But now, I think it's almost 100 percent As crazy as this might sound, probably close to 100 percent of the people watched our games with Texas and Kansas.

"It's been amazing to see the community lift itself up around this. We've always gotten a lot of attention, I know that. But now it's doubled. At least. So now, everybody's into it. I mean, everybody. People who never watched us play before have taken possession of this team."

Boeheim might have been right. And for support of this, I offer—with your presumed indulgence—a personal story.

It was my great honor to cover the 2003 Final Four, my 20th such assignment, for the *Syracuse Post-Standard* newspaper and for the loyal readers of that grand publication. And I looked forward to sharing the experience with my bride of nearly a quarter-century once I got home from Louisiana.

Now, Kathleen's a great gal. Fetching. Intelligent. Good-humored. But a team sports fan, she is not. And, excepting our kids' athletic careers, a team sports fan she'd never been. But I wasn't in the house for 10 minutes before I was given Kathleen's equivalent of Boeheim's big loony hat.

"I was so wound up last night, I couldn't sleep after I went to bed," she said, as my jaw began to drop like a southbound dumb-waiter. "I was so nervous. I thought they were going to lose there at the end. I'm telling you, I was in knots. And then Hakim blocked that shot!"

You must understand that in the 25-plus years I'd known this woman, I'd never heard her discuss a game, and I'd never seen her watch a game that did not involve our son, Nathan, or our daughter, Caitlin. Never.

But on that April evening in 2003, everything changed.

"That Gerry McNamara was so good," Kathleen told me. "He didn't miss a shot. And Carmelo Anthony was amazing. And that zone defense SU played! Those Kansas guys couldn't even shoot it."

And with that—and, if I'm lying, may God sentence me to an eternal airplane flight planted in a middle seat in coach next to Dick Vitale—Kathleen assumed a defensive stance, with hands up, right there in our living room.

"Who," I finally blurted, "are you?"

Turns out, she was just another of the happily afflicted. That's who Kathleen was. And she stood in a very, very long line.

Fact is, though, the Orangemen have been playing this game for more than 100 years, and not just since Carmelo Anthony and his cuddly band came along. Which means there is a century and more of SU basketball tales wafting within the memory banks of those who played and observed, who listened and remembered. And this book—virtually all of which deals with recollections culled in the two months following Syracuse's 81-78 win over Kansas in the Superdome—has captured just a few.

I had my fun stringing together everybody's stories, which are presented on the pages that follow pretty much in chronological order. Here's hoping you have your fun reading them. If you do so from beneath a big loony hat, all the better.

Bud Poliquin
July 2003

They started playing basketball at Syracuse University in 1901, or back when William McKinley was running the country. Beginning with the Orangemen's 23-8 loss to Rensselaer Polytechnic Institute on January 5 of that year and continuing through SU's 81-78 national title-game triumph over Kansas on April 7, 2003, a total of 470 players had earned varsity basketball letters at the school on the big hill in town.

Twenty-nine of them, including the most recent, Carmelo Anthony, went on to play in the NBA. Others, however, walked down different paths. Some became NFL stars, others became FBI agents, still others became schoolteachers. There is a doctor and a dentist on the list. And a city's chief of police, too. One became the first African-American to win football's Heisman Trophy and another became a major-league baseball pitcher and another became a Vietnam War hero-turned-Methodist minister. There are lawyers among them. And salesmen. And coaches. And so much more.

They've fanned out, as well, living as far west as California, as far south as Florida, as far north as the Dakotas and as far east as Maine. And they've gone global with some settling in places like Sweden and the Virgin Islands and Bosnia and Puerto Rico.

There have been a whole bunch of them, that's for sure. From A to Z—excepting the letters I, U and X. And because Dick Ableman and Mark Ziolko suited up for Syracuse just five years apart, that A-to-Z business can be taken literally.

"I guess I'm at the head of the class," said Ableman. "Maybe not academically, but alphabetically."

"I suppose if you have to get yourself distinguished," said Ziolko, "being the last guy on the list is one way to do it."

Ableman? He was a six-foot-three jack-of-all-trades who played from 1963-64 through '65-66 for Orange clubs that went 52-24. Ziolko? He was a six-foot-eight center who played from 1970-71 through '71-72 for Syracuse teams that finished 41-13. Both, then, had their fun.

"We had a fellow on the team named Dave Bing," said Ableman, who came to SU from suburban Albany, N.Y., and now is a sales manager in Gainesville, Georgia. "And he pretty much did whatever he wanted to do. We were a fast-breaking team and we put the ball in Dave's hands, because usually good things happened when we did.

"And Jim Boeheim was part of that group, too. His personality back then wasn't exactly vivacious, you know what I mean? But I will say this for him: Jim got more out of his ability than anybody I ever played with. Structurally, he was pretty much physically challenged. But, boy, was he smart. And he always played so hard."

Though Ziolko's career was cut short by a knee injury suffered at Madison Square Garden's ECAC Holiday Festival during his junior season, he's held onto his memories... even if most of them deal with his time spent as the backup to Bill Smith, the six-foot-11 starter who averaged 20.7 points and 12.9 rebounds during his three-year Orange career that ended in '71.

"After Smith, we were 'Roy's Runts,' because Mike Lee, at six-foot-three, was our power forward and Mark Wadach, at six-foot-one, was our small forward," said Ziolko, who arrived at SU from Orchard Park, N.Y., and now works for the city of Syracuse. "And Wadach almost led our team in rebounding. We had a small lineup, but I'd like to think that was the start of the Orange program that has carried over to this day. I enjoyed going along for the ride."

From the "Z" spot in the order, that is. Or 469 names after that of Ableman up there in the "A" position.

Ableman . . . Ziolko. Syracuse lettermen, both. In the truest sense of the word.

THE OTHER CHAMPIONS

The good citizens of central and upstate New York properly went crazy watching the 2002-03 Orangemen play their way to both a 30-5 record and the NCAA Tournament championship. But those who'd believed that Carmelo Anthony and Co. had delivered Syracuse University's first national basketball title were wrong.

Nah, the school produced two other championship teams, both of which have been pretty much lost in time's long shadows. The first of those, the 1917-18 Orangemen, went 16-1, losing only to Pennsylvania, 17-16, in their season finale. SU's other title bunch posted a 19-1 record in 1925-26 and lost only to Penn State, 37-31.

Fact is, neither of those Orange clubs actually won its crown on the court in the kind of tournament format with which we are so familiar today. No, they were anointed retroactively by the Helms Foundation of Los Angeles, whose founder, Bill Schroeder, also named All-America teams and Hall of Fame inductees.

That 1917-18 outfit was led by Joe Schwartzer and Leon Marcus, each of whom later became Helms Foundation All-Americans. Meanwhile, the star of the 1925-26 squad was SU legend Vic Hanson, who remains the only player to be inducted into both the Naismith Memorial Basketball and College Football halls of fame . . . even if his favorite game had always been baseball.

There are, of course, few among us who are old enough to have seen any of those marvelous Orangemen perform, but Murray Bernthal is one such lucky gent. And he'll not soon forget what he observed.

"Vic Hanson was terrific," said Bernthal, who was 92 when these tales went to print. "He seemed to take three steps between dribbles. I've never seen a guy run so fast. And he was so canny. He was really good, but you have to remember that basketball was a lot different in those days.

"You didn't have a game where somebody went down the floor all by himself, dribbling behind his back and making a play. It wasn't like that. Back then people took the ball down court together, crisscrossing as they went. And the defense made you make a play before you crossed the foul line. It wasn't better basketball; it was different basketball. And that's the kind of ball Vic Hanson played."

Bernthal, who graduated from SU in 1932 and played briefly on the school's freshman basketball team, knows of what he speaks. Though he's served continuously since 1942 as the executive director of Famous Artists, the company that continues to bring Broadway stage productions to downtown Syracuse, Bernthal has followed sports as passionately as he has arts and the theater.

And high on his list of memorable athletes is the five-foot-11 Vic Hanson, the old lineman who actually became the head coach of the Orange football team for seven years in the 1930s, leading it to a record of 33-21-5.

"Vic wasn't sweet, but he was affable," said Bernthal, who also played on SU's tennis team for two seasons. "He spoke to everybody. We've had guys on the teams up there who did not make friends off the court. You know, guys who were too big for their britches and wouldn't sign autographs and things like that. But not Vic Hanson. He was wonderful."

And he was a national basketball champion fully 77 years before Carmelo Anthony became one himself.

OH, THE REINDEER FIVE COULD PLAY

It didn't take long for Murray Bernthal, one of Syracuse's more remarkable citizens, to see the proverbial writing on the wall in 1928. So, he grabbed his violin and skedaddled.

Newly arrived on the SU campus back when Calvin Coolidge was in the White House, Bernthal was a five-foot-nine guard from Brooklyn on an athletic half-scholarship that was worth, roughly, $120. And no, that's not a joke.

Soon, though, Murray was on a full ride, at a princely $240 . . . but off the Orange basketball team. And it was all because of The Reindeer Five, so dubbed because they were small and fast—the Donners and Blitzens of their time.

"They turned out to be one of the greatest teams in Syracuse history," declared Bernthal, who was born in 1911 and can talk just as easily about Vic Hanson as Carmelo Anthony. "It was Kenny Beagle. And Ev Katz. And Tuppy Hayman, who was a wonderful shooter. And Slim Elliott, who was a giant center of, maybe, five-foot-11. And Dan Fogarty, who was strong, but didn't have a lot of push.

"Well, I've got to tell you, I wasn't great, but I was pretty good. And I found myself sitting on the bench one day watching them. Watching the Reindeer Five. And I thought, 'If I stick around here, with these guys ahead of me, I'll never play.' You know, I'd toured the country as a classical violinist before I went to SU, so I got myself a violin audition and when it was over, I had a full music scholarship. And that was the end of my basketball career at Syracuse."

It turns out that Bernthal did stick around the campus for a while, joining the SU faculty in 1932 and staying for 46 years, teaching string instruments, ensemble and music methods to students who hoped to become teachers themselves.

And the Reindeer Five? Coached by the often-ornery and always parsimonious Lew Andreas, they peaked during the 1929-30 season when they went 18-2, losing their two games—at Creighton and at Columbia—by a total of seven points.

BILLY GABOR'S PIONEER DAYS

The folks up there at Syracuse University proudly refer to the Carrier Dome as "the finest all-purpose on-campus sports facility in the nation." And with its near-50,000 seats for football and its 33,000-plus seats for basketball, it very well could be.

But the guys in the sneakers, specifically, didn't always have it so good.

"Let's just put it this way," said Billy Gabor. "The places we played in weren't the Dome. You know what I mean?"

As Gabor—who led the Orangemen in scoring in each of his four varsity seasons back in the 1940s—is now on the far side of 80, he'd know.

Indeed, back in the day—that is, "Bullet" Billy Gabor's day—SU suited up in Archbold Gym, the Jefferson Street Armory and the State Fairgrounds Coliseum, with the odd game tossed in at the downtown Onondaga County War Memorial. It wasn't until 1962 that Manley Field House (with all its dirt and dust) opened, and that was abandoned in 1980 for the spiffy Dome.

"I didn't have a favorite building," said Gabor, who was a five-foot-11 forward (yes, forward). "You have to play the cards you're dealt, so wherever they sent us, we had to play well. We were like vagabonds in our own town."

Archbold Gym? Home to the Orangemen between 1908-1947 (and again from 1952-1955), it seated some 3,000, was circled by a running track, and was damaged by a fire soon after the end of World War II. The Armory? It had a capacity of around 2,500 and was better known for the drills held within its walls by the Army and Army Reserves. The Coliseum? Perhaps 6,000 people could squeeze into it…and when they did, the smoke from their cigars, cigarettes, and pipes made seeing the floor from the faraway pews a red-eyed challenge.

"None of those places was really very good," said Gabor, a Helms Foundation All-American who scored 1,344 points as an Orangeman. "They had hot water, but otherwise the locker rooms were pretty bad. I mean, they didn't really have lockers. There were just hangers for your clothes and nails in the wall for the coats. But that's how it was in those days, the pioneer days."

Beyond the arenas, there was at least one more indicator that Gabor and his teammates were far removed from the 21st century. That would be in the area of sports medicine, whose practitioners were apparently just a few years beyond the use of leeches.

"One day, I sprained my ankle really bad and they put me in the infirmary," recalled Gabor, whose SU basketball career was interrupted by a two-year stint as an Air Force bombardier. "For my therapy, they had me stick my foot in a half wooden-barrel thing with a 300-watt light bulb inside. Then, they'd turn on the light and put a sheet over the top of the barrel to hold the heat in. And that was it. That was the extent of the treatment.

"So, we're playing Colgate the next day and Lew Andreas, the coach, comes to see me. 'How's the ankle?' he asks. I say, 'I haven't walked on it, so I don't know.' 'Well, you're a tough kid. Give it a try.' So, he sends me off to the trainer. The trainer gives me a shot of Novocain, tapes up my ankle and I play. We go off and beat Colgate, they untape my ankle after the game, and I still can't walk. And I ended up back in the infirmary. Like I said, those were the pioneer days."

Happily, Gabor survived them. More than that, he thrived during them and landed in the NBA with the old

Syracuse Nationals for whom he played seven seasons. Why, he remains one of only six players under six feet in height—along with Michael Adams, Dana Barros, Ralph Beard, Calvin Murphy and Fred Scolari—to have played in an NBA All-Star Game, which is something Billy did in 1953.

He's proud of that feat, and for good reason. But the fact is, Billy Gabor, the famed "Bullet" out of Binghamton, N.Y., is more agog at what he eyes in front of him than what he gazes upon in the rear-view mirror.

"I've been to the Dome," he said while seated in his beachside home in Jupiter, Florida. "And when I'm there, I can't believe what I'm looking at. When I think of where we played and then I walk around that place with 30,000 fans in it . . . well, when you get to be 81 like me, you just don't expect to see stuff like that."

He is a pioneer from the pioneer days, that's what Billy is. Allow him, then, to be amazed.

GOOD MAN...CANTANKEROUS COACH

He certainly wasn't the cuddly type. Not Lew Andreas, who'd growl—and that's to be taken literally—at missed free throws, blown assignments and tardy arrivals. But the man was a beacon back in the '40s if you were six-foot-eight and weary of being a sideshow.

And Royce Newell was both.

"With Lew Andreas, if you were a big guy, you weren't supposed to be a plodding freak out there on the court," said Newell. "You were expected to be mobile. You were expected to be more than a rebounder at the back end of a fast break."

Be advised that Andreas was ahead of his time. And Newell, the proverbial long drink of water at six-foot-eight and 185 pounds, was delighted. He was allowed, after all, to be a basketball player and not just another gangly act yanked from a midway tent. And everybody won.

Andreas, the old Syracuse coach and Helms Foundation Hall of Famer, was Jim Boeheim before Jim Boeheim, going 358-135 in 25 seasons (22 of which were winning ones) between 1924-25 and 1949-50. And he put those numbers together with an inventive run-and-gun style that made stars out of Vic Hanson and the Reindeer Five and "Bullet" Billy Gabor.

He also made a loyalist out of Royce Newell, now living in retirement in Camillus, N.Y., after having served for so long as a high school teacher, coach and athletic director (even if he did earn only $2,500 in his first year on the job).

"Lew could be cantankerous," said Newell, who'd come to SU from Jamestown, N.Y., and went 71-30 in his four-year varsity career. "Yes, he could. He had things in his mind that he wanted done, and he wanted them done his way. But he was a good man. There is no question about that."

Evidently, Andreas, who also served as SU's AD between 1937-64, was a sterling coach as well. He led the Orangemen to a 54-8 record in his first 62 games on the job and to a 36-16 record in his final 52 before giving way—at the age of 55—to his assistant, Marc Guley. And along the way, he had campaigns of 23-4, 19-1, 19-6, 18-2, 18-7, 18-9, 16-4, 15-2, 15-2, 15-2, 15-4 and 14-2. And if, on his watch, SU scored only seven points in a 1932 loss at Creighton…well, it's only fair to report that it did put up, under his gaze, 105 in a 1950 conquest of Temple.

"You couldn't say the players were dedicated to him," suggested Newell, who arrived on campus in 1945 with a broken heart after he'd been deemed too tall (by two inches) to serve in the military. "He wasn't a Bobby Knight, by any stretch. But you didn't throw your arms around Lew Andreas. And you never picked him up and carried him off on your shoulders.

"But he could coach. He didn't believe in set plays, but we did run a three-man weave and sometimes a four-man weave. And at the end, we were using a double-post, high and low. You know who reminds me of him? Eddie Sutton of Oklahoma State, that's who. You know how Sutton always has that scowl on his face and is very demanding? That was Lew Andreas."

One imagines that Andreas, whose voice grew raspier by the year, must have frowned often on Christmas Eve, 1947, as he accompanied his Orangemen from Syracuse to Los Angeles for a holiday tournament—via an 18-hour series of flights that had stops in Rochester, Buffalo, Erie, Akron, Louisville and Memphis.

And, yeah, he probably even growled a bit en route.

"That's what he did when he wasn't happy," said Newell of his beacon, who died at 88 in 1983. "Lew growled. And, sure, he growled at me occasionally. And when he did, he was right."

Royce was six-foot-eight, remember, in a five-foot-eight world. And Lew Andreas allowed him—no, demanded of him—to be a basketball freak no more. As such, forgive Newell, an oddity because he ran rather than lumbered, for remembering that his old coach's growling sounded more like a melody.

"WHAT ARE YOU TRYING TO DO?
WE'RE THE PROS!"

He was only a sophomore in the fall of 1951, a kid out of Manlius Military School who could shoot from anywhere just inside the county line. But already, Mel Besdin was deep into his basketball education.

For openers, he'd only recently learned that Syracuse was not going to hire the "big-name" coach he'd heard about during his recruitment. Marc Guley, whose first year on the job had been as the "interim" head coach, had choreographed a 19-9 record there during the 1950-51 campaign. And his Orangemen had closed the season by winning the prestigious National Campus Tournament in Peoria, Illinois— beating Toledo, Utah and scandal-ridden Bradley by a total of 35 points—to thus end his maiden voyage at the head of the SU bench on a 10-1 run.

So, Guley—a Ph.D. who coached the golf team and taught classes, in addition to ramrodding the Orange basketeers (all for a salary of $6,500)—had earned the right to erase the word, "interim," from his title. For, it turned out down the road, worse rather than for better.

Secondly, Besdin, a six-foot-three guard, gazed upon the NBA from such close range that he could smell the socks— and he came away amazed.

"So, there I am," Mel recalled. "It's October, I'm in my first year on the varsity, we haven't played a game yet…and we get the word that the Syracuse Nationals want to raise some funds. So, they ask Guley if he's interested in a charity game."

Yeah, that's right. The very same Nationals who'd come within three points of advancing to the NBA Finals the previous season, wanted to take on the Orangemen at the Onondaga County War Memorial. And Besdin was agog.

"You've got to remember," he said. "This was Syracuse. And when it came to sports, the Nats were everything."

Those Nats suited up Dolph Schayes, who'd led the NBA in rebounding with his 16.4 average the previous year. And they also dressed the likes of Red Rocha, George King, Paul Seymour and former Orangeman Billy Gabor. And they were used to butting heads with George Mikan and Bob Cousy and Paul Arizin and Harry "The Horse" Gallatin, not with any bunch of college boys.

As such, it was going to be a walkover. A rout. A New York Yankees-vs.-Washington Senators kind of thing. But it wasn't.

"The War Memorial was pretty much full, and at half-time we were beating them," Besdin remembered. "Well, Danny Biasone (the Nats' owner) and Al Cervi (their player/coach) come into our locker room, and they start to yell at Guley.

"They're screaming, 'What are you trying to do? We're the pros!' We were laughing hysterically. I mean, they had Dolph Schayes and all those other guys. The truth is, it was early in the preseason and they weren't really ready to play, and we'd gotten lucky. They came back to beat us in the second half. But, man, they were furious."

And what of Besdin, who'd end up as the Orangemen's captain as a senior? Back then, all he could do was shake his head.

"That was my first taste of honey," Mel said. "I remember thinking, 'Goodness gracious. Does this go on all the time?' I've got to say, it was quite an introduction to the varsity."

And it was quite a send-off for the season, too. In 1951-52, Guley's Orangemen won their first six games, climbed to as high as No. 14 in the polls and finished with a record of 14-6. The Nats, meanwhile, won the NBA's Eastern Division with a 40-26 record and advanced again to the conference finals.

Oh, and Biasone and Cervi did simmer down.

THE FOOTBALL FACTOR

Squint into the distance at Syracuse University's football Mount Rushmore and whose likenesses do you see carved into the vast granite wall? Certainly, Jim Brown, who became by acclamation the greatest running back the game has ever seen. Absolutely, Ernie Davis, the first African-American to win the Heisman Trophy. Probably, John Mackey, who evolved into the prototype tight end and a Pro Football Hall of Famer. And likely, Donovan McNabb, the quarterback who, in 2002, signed the richest deal—12 years, $115 million—ever awarded a football player.

Jim Brown. Ernie Davis. John Mackey. Donovan McNabb. As every central and upstate New York schoolchild knows, each was an Orange football star. But what that little boy or girl might not understand is that each of those fellows played varsity basketball at SU, too.

"I loved basketball," said Brown, who was speaking from his handsome home in the hills above Los Angeles. "We had some pretty good teams when I was at Syracuse. And I could play a little. I averaged something like 38 points a game in high school. I could run, I could jump, I could shoot."

If it's the truth, it ain't bragging and Jim Brown—who was brilliant in football, stunning in lacrosse, formidable in track and field, terrific in baseball and fearsome enough with his fists to be deemed, by SU boxing coach Roy Simmons, Sr., a future heavyweight champion—was hardly bragging.

Moreover, a look at the available basketball statistics during their times as Orangemen indicates that Brown, who'd come to town from Long Island's Manhasset High School (where he'd earned 13 varsity letters), was the best of football's Big Four:

—Brown (1954-55 through 1955-56): 43 games, 13.1 ppg.

—Davis (1960-61): 9 games, 10.2 ppg, 9.6 rpg.

—Mackey (1960-61): 6 games, 4.7 ppg, 4.7 rpg.

—McNabb (1995-96 through 1996-97): 18 games, 2.3 ppg, 1.1 rpg, 0.4 apg.

Unfortunately, though, Brown did not play as a senior. Nearly 50 years later, the man remained insistent that it was his desire to suit up. But he just couldn't.

"My basketball experience at Syracuse was really very bad," Brown said. "What happened was that Marc Guley was the coach and it was a terrible situation. I didn't play anymore because of him. I wanted to play, and the guys on the team asked me to come back, but it was impossible. I told them I couldn't deal with the coach, so it made sense for me not to get involved."

Guley, who died in 1990, coached at SU for 12 seasons, from 1950-51 through 1961-62. But after winning 34 of his first 49 games at the head of the Orange bench, he lost 43 of his last 49 games in that seat and was replaced by Fred Lewis.

The sorry truth is, Guley struggled with more than a few issues while on the job. And one of them was his ability to get along with certain athletes.

"Jim was a tremendous player," said Manny Breland, who was Brown's teammate for one season. "Marc Guley has passed on and you don't want to say bad things, so I'll just put it this way: He was not sensitive to black men. I don't know that he was a racist; it's just that he couldn't deal with blacks. As a result, we had several guys who left, and Jim was one of them.

"We just didn't respect Guley the way you'd think players would respect a Division I coach, particularly after we saw guys like Frank McGuire from North Carolina. He'd come in with the blazer on and the white hair coiffed so fine. He had his necktie and his shirt just so. I mean, he was the personification of a Division I coach. And in our minds, for a lot of reasons, Guley didn't measure up."

And so, Brown walked away. And both Davis (who was better known at Elmira Free Academy for this basketball abilities than for his football prowess) and Mackey hung up their sneakers following SU's disastrous 4-19 campaign in 1960-61, which means those two missed the 2-22 debacle that followed.

"We all felt that if we had Jim when he was a senior, the results would have been completely different," said Breland. "He could have averaged 15-16 points and 10 rebounds a game for us. He was just a phenomenal athlete who could do anything and everything well. We could have really used him that year."

Well, sure. That was the 1956-57 season during which the Orangemen lost to undefeated North Carolina, 67-58, in the Elite 8 of the NCAA Tournament. Which, of course, was the season the Tar Heels won the national championship with their triple-overtime conquest of Wilt Chamberlain's Kansas Jayhawks in the title game.

So, yes, with a little imagination it's possible to see Jim Brown driving against Wilt Chamberlain—think of a seven-foot-one Sam Huff—with college basketball's crown on the line.

But it wasn't meant to be.

"Like I said, we had some good teams," Brown said. "We had Manny. We had Vinnie Cohen. We had guys who were really fast and could really jump. We beat a lot of people. But I wasn't at Syracuse on a basketball scholarship and I just didn't want to deal with the coach. So, that was it."

As such, Jim Brown settled on football. As did Davis and Mackey and McNabb, whose decisions landed them with Brown on SU's imaginary Mount Rushmore. Which begs the question: If an in-their-prime Brown and McNabb took on an in-their-prime Davis and Mackey in a two-on-two game in the driveway, on whom would you bet lunch?

Better make that a best-of-three.

JIM BROWN, THE ADONIS

Though he became known as perhaps the greatest running back the game of football has ever seen, Jim Brown was more than that. Why, given his corresponding prowess in lacrosse, baseball, and track and field, and acknowledging his promise as a boxer, the argument can be made that Brown was the most accomplished athlete the world has ever known.

Hey, somebody's got to be No. 1, right? Why not James Nathaniel Brown, who—in addition to everything else—also played two seasons of varsity basketball at Syracuse University in the mid-1950s and averaged 13.1 points in the 43 games in which he participated?

"He was," said Mel Besdin, "unbelievable."

Be advised that Besdin—who was a senior on the SU basketball team when Brown was a member of the Orange freshman club—knows his subject. After all, back then, during the 1953-54 season, the varsity periodically scrimmaged the frosh. Which means that the six-foot-three Besdin, the Orangemen's captain and leading scorer (16.1), regularly encountered the six-foot-two Brown on the floor.

But it was in the locker room where Besdin first gulped at the sight of the Georgia-born manchild who would soon become, as a rampaging Cleveland Brown, every NFL defender's nightmare.

"I'll remember this for as long as I live," proclaimed Besdin. "We're all in the shower, taking our showers, and Jimmy Brown walks in. He's a freshman, don't forget. A 17-year-old freshman. And he comes in there with a 29-inch waist and these huge shoulders and these huge legs. We looked at him, just standing there…and we basically said, 'Oh, my God.'

"Here we were, a bunch of varsity athletes. And here was this kid. I'm telling you, he was 17! And we looked at each other and said, 'Man, are we inadequate or what? We must be kidding ourselves.' I swear, Jimmy looked like Adonis. We all walked out of there with our heads hanging."

MANNY BRELAND'S LITTLE MIRACLE

The 2003 NCAA Tournament, the one that has already become a mental heirloom for Syracuse basketball fans, was the 28th such grand event in which the Orangemen had participated. In Jim Boeheim's 27-year tenure alone, SU had gone to 22 NCAA tournaments. So March Madness has pretty much become a presupposed fever in central and upstate New York.

But such was not always the case. In fact, Syracuse did not qualify for any of the initial 18 NCAA Tournaments. And so, from 1939-1956, the hoop landscape in late winter was fairly barren in Orange Nation.

Oh, there were two NIT appearances, in 1946 and 1950. And although those ended fairly quickly with respective losses to Muhlenberg and Bradley, they were fine. But nothing was doing on the NCAA Tournament front until 1957, which was when SU finally broke through.

In a happy twist of fate, Manny Breland was in a Syracuse uniform instead of out in the world making a buck.

"I should have graduated in 1956," said Breland, "but I got sick and missed what was supposed to have been my senior year. So I came back...and guess what? We had our best season and made the NCAA Tournament. For me, it was kind of like a little miracle."

Some miracle. Manny, you see, was diagnosed in the summer of 1955 with tuberculosis while at ROTC camp in Fort Bragg, N.C., and underwent a kind of pioneering surgery on a lung that fall. Hence he sat out a year while recuperating. Thus, he was, ahem, blessed.

"To this day," said Breland, who is living in retirement in Syracuse after a long and fruitful career as an educator and coach, "I've looked upon my illness as an act of Providence."

He was a six-foot-three guard for the Orangemen during their 16-6 regular season and his medical condition didn't allow him to breathe out there on the floor; rather, Manny gasped. And nothing changed in the Tournament.

"We were playing Connecticut in the first round at Madison Square Garden," said Breland, a Syracuse native who'd attended old Central High School in the city. "It was a back-and-forth game and I couldn't control my breathing. Several times I got called for palming the ball because I'd be dribbling and then my bad breathing would interrupt things. So, I'd have to stop and catch my breath, and I'd end up carrying the ball."

Manny's problem ended up being only a nuisance for the Orangemen, who defeated the Huskies, 82-76, and then eliminated Lafayette, 75-71, in the second round. Next up, however, was North Carolina, complete with its overpowering height, a 29-0 record, and its All-American, Lennie Rosenbluth.

And just like that, SU came to the end of its first NCAA Tournament road, losing to the Tar Heels, 67-58, after being outscored by 23 points (33-10) at the foul line.

"Rosenbluth was a wiry guy with rapier-like elbows," recalled Breland. "Well, we're all running down the court at one point and—I'll never forget this for as long as I live—Rosenbluth elbowed one of our forwards, Jim Snyder, right in the stomach. I don't know what happened, but Jim turned green. I mean, he was really hurting. And that took us right out of the game."

With the win, North Carolina advanced to the Final Four where it eventually defeated Wilt Chamberlain's Kansas team in that triple-overtime epic to finish undefeated at 32-0. And the Orangemen? They went home with their 18-7 record and with the knowledge that they'd been the first SU club to venture so deep into March.

And Manny Breland, whose bad health had led to good times, was there. Gasping, yes, but otherwise enjoying nearly every minute. Thanks, quite possibly, to Providence.

One "Funny" Rule Cost a Title

As far as Vinnie Cohen is concerned, Don Haskins's bold decision to start an all-African-American basketball team down there at Texas Western was made a decade too late.

You remember—it was 1966. The NCAA title game. Haskins's upstart Miners vs. Adolph Rupp's blue-blooded (and Caucasian) Kentucky Wildcats. And so many eyes were fixed upon College Park, Maryland, because uppity Texas Western was breaking the unwritten and unspoken—but apparently very much understood—rule of the college basketball road.

"Before Texas Western came along," said Cohen, "the understanding was that teams would not start more than two African-Americans. After that game, real integration came into the sport. But it was too late for us. I've always believed that Syracuse would have won the national championship in my senior year if not for that funny rule."

That would have been the 1956-57 season during which the Orangemen went 18-7 and lost to North Carolina in the contest that would have propelled SU into the Final Four. That would have been the year, more specifically, after a disgusted Jim Brown got up and left.

"Jim quit the team because of that rule," Cohen said. "He would have brought at least 15 points and 10 rebounds with him every game that season, and that would have been enough to get us to the finals and the national title. But Manny Breland and I were the two black starters, and Jim saw the unfairness and he just wouldn't accept it."

So, having returned to the football field—and the lacrosse pitch, too—the wondrous Brown was gone. And the Orangemen, even with talents such as Cohen and Breland

and Jon Cincebox and Gary Clark and Jim Snyder and Larry Loudis, were destined to come up one man short. And they did.

"It really wasn't so much Marc Guley's fault," said Cohen, in reference to SU's head coach at the time. "It was the way of America then. I always thought sports were sort of pure. If you can run faster than me, then you win the 100-yard dash, you know? But that's not the way it was in basketball. It hurt the university, and I think the university knows that now. But it was the custom in those days, the practice. Syracuse just went along to get along, I guess."

It was a shame, because that Orange bunch was awfully good, putting together an 18-4 run that included a double-overtime loss, a two-point defeat and a five-point setback among those four failures. And the catalyst was Cohen, a six-foot-one guard out of Boys High School in Brooklyn who averaged 24.2 points per game, a figure that has been topped only twice at SU since the end of World War II—by Dave Bing in 1965-66 (28.4) and by Greg Kohls in 1971-72 (26.7).

Still, SU almost lost Cohen, who'd enrolled as a freshman with Brown in 1953 and, like Brown, was a hugely gifted 17-year-old without benefit of an athletic scholarship.

"Funny, isn't it?" said Cohen. "The guy who would become the star of the football team doesn't have a scholarship. And the guy who would become the star of the basketball team doesn't have a scholarship. And both are told that if they 'prove' themselves, they'll get scholarships. Interesting, huh?

"In my case, I was thinking, 'Goodness gracious.' I mean, a lot of the guys that got scholarships were six-foot-nine and six-foot-ten. But if you can't walk or run or catch, it really doesn't make any difference how tall you are. I led the freshman team in scoring. Wouldn't you think I 'proved' myself by doing that? But even then, they were hemming and hawing about giving me a scholarship. Same with Jim."

As a result, both Cohen (who was bound for St. John's) and Brown decided to transfer, but each was persuaded to stay when scholarships ultimately materialized. And each became luminaries—Cohen, first, as an All-America basketball player who led the Orangemen in scoring in each of his three varsity seasons and, later, as a Washington, D.C., lawyer for 40 years...and Brown, first, as perhaps the greatest athlete ever produced by the human race and, later, as a noted social activist.

So, things turned out well. Sort of.

"For me, Syracuse was a very mixed experience," said Cohen. "I'm glad I got my education there. I mean, the university—and after that, the Syracuse School of Law—gave me my paycheck. But outside of that, it really was a tragedy the way athletics were handled there at the time.

"I'm happy that Syracuse won the national championship. I like Carmelo Anthony and I like Jim Boeheim, and that team really played like a team. But we could have won the title ourselves a long time ago. And if it wasn't for that rule—if Jim Brown had stayed on the team and played—I think we would have."

Somewhere, Don Haskins sighs.

THE NAME (AND PRESUMPTION) GAME

What's in a name? Vinnie Cohen will tell ya what's in a name. He'll tell ya that what's mostly in a name is a whole lot of presumption. Take this one-question test and see for yourself:

When you hear the name, "Vinnie Cohen," you think of:

(a) A Jewish tailor.

(b) A Jewish lawyer. Or,

(c) A black (and Episcopalian-raised) All-America basketball player.

You might be inclined to disregard (c) and consider only (a) and (b). And you'd be wrong.

"When I'd get introduced before games, there would be gasps from the fans," said Cohen, who was, once upon a time, every bit (c). "People didn't know what to think. I mean, Vinnie Cohen is such a Jewish name, and here was this African-American kid running around out on the court."

Make no mistake that there was some confusion when Cohen, a six-foot-one guard, was starring for the Orangemen back in the 1950s. By any name, though, he was a player—scoring 1,337 points in his three-year varsity career, averaging 19.7 points in the 68 games in which he played, and leading Syracuse to a cumulative record of 42-26.

"I asked my dad about it one day," Cohen recalled. "I said, 'Dad, how'd we get this name?' Now, you need to know that he was from the Caribbean and he wasn't a very talkative guy. And he told me, 'My dad, your grandfather, was a rabbi.' And that was it. I said, 'Oh, that makes sense.' So I told everybody, and they backed off.

"I don't really know if it's true, but my father didn't joke around. A Jewish friend of mine used to say, 'Do some research and find out what's going on.' And I told him, 'Man, I've got enough problems as it is. I don't need to be Jewish. I'm black. That's trouble enough.' I mean, Jewish people were catching hell. So, I wasn't interested one way or the other."

Vinnie Cohen, then, was clearly (c). But after graduation, he did attend the Syracuse School of Law. And he did become a high-powered attorney, hanging his shingle in Washington, D.C., for 40 years. Which, come to think of it, could have made him, over all this time, (b) in addition to (c). That is, if his father was giving it to him straight.

So much for presumption.

2-22

With the 2003 NCAA Tournament title in the bag, the Orangemen walked out of the Louisiana Superdome on April 7, 2003, with 1,607 victories dating back to the school's inaugural basketball season of 1901. That's a lot of wins spread over a lot of years, a fact supported by this one: Only Kentucky (1,849), North Carolina (1,807), Kansas (1,801), Duke (1,706), St. John's (1,660) and Temple (by a single triumph at 1,608) had accumulated more among Division I teams.

But not every Syracuse campaign has been, as Al McGuire used to say, about seashells and balloons. Not every bunch of Orangemen has beamed in the manner of Carmelo Anthony and his starry teammates. Not every SU basketball experience has been a charmed one.

Take, for instance, 1961-62. Please.

"That," said Manny Klutschkowski, "was not a lot of fun."

"It was a struggle," said Carl Vernick. "A big struggle."

How limited was the fun? How big was the struggle? The Orangemen went 2-22 that year—losing by 63 to NYU, by 37 to DePaul, by 32 to Niagara, by 29 to St. John's, by 28 to Detroit, by 28 to Manhattan, by 28 to Canisius, by 23 to Massachusetts...you get the idea. They dropped 22 contests in a row to start the season. They endured a nation's worst 27-game losing streak that had begun during the previous campaign. They were pounded in back-to-back nights at the Motor City Tournament by a total of 65 points.

"You know, it wasn't that we weren't trying," said Klutschkowski, who was SU's six-foot-six center and its leading rebounder at 6.8 boards per game. "It's kind of stuck in my craw after all these years. Those were the down times of

Syracuse basketball, and I was part of it. So, I don't feel real good when I talk about it. But I did what I could do. I tried my best. The truth is, we just didn't have a very good team."

Those Orangemen were thin, all right. Three key players—Loren James, Ernie Lotano and Billy Connors (yeah, the baseball Billy Connors)—ran into eligibility problems and did not return from the preceding season. And their coach, Marc Guley, was in the final campaign of his 12-year run that had begun with the promise of a 19-9 effort in 1950-51 but had unraveled to the point of embarrassment, both on the court and off.

"At one point," recalled Vernick, a six-foot-two guard who led Syracuse in scoring with his 16.5 average during that 1961-62 disaster, "Guley turned to Herb Foster, the team captain, and said, 'You pick out the starting lineup. You can do it better than me.' It became hard to watch because Guley was suffering. But what were we supposed to do? We were dealt a bad hand. A lot of our bus rides home were quiet as tombs."

Happily, though—no, shockingly—the misery did end with smiles, because the Orangemen managed to win their final two affairs—on the road, yet—at Boston College, 73-72, and at Connecticut, 72-67. And the Eagles (15-7) and the Huskies (16-8) were both pretty good.

"I remember that BC game, sure," said Vernick, who was a sophomore at the time and currently runs his own drilling and testing company on Long Island. "It was tight to the final seconds. Somehow I got a breakaway layup near the end of the game and as I was racing down the court with the ball, the guys on the bench were standing and cheering. When I laid it in, you know, it was a great feeling. A great, great feeling."

More than that, Vernick's basket helped to halt the humiliating streak that had lasted from February 20, 1961 until March 3, 1962—a stretch of one year, one week and four days between victories for the Syracuse guys. And it nicely set things up for their equally amazing win over UConn two nights later.

"I think that shows you something about that team," said Klutschkowski, who was then a junior but is now a retired schoolteacher in Newport, N.Y. "Those were tough times. The freshmen used to kick our tails at every single practice. Daily. I mean, *daily.* But we didn't give up. We just kept playing. When you go through years like that, nothing is really a highlight. But those two wins sure were."

Of course they were. You see, the Orangemen didn't really start their season 0-22; they finished it 2-0.

THE BEST ORANGEMAN
THERE EVER WAS

The kid's name was Wally Goodwin, and he was nothing if not a measuring stick.

"He was six-foot-one and, man, could he jump," said Sam Penceal. "He was one of those guys with great big thighs and thin lower legs. I'm telling you, he was amazing. He could really get up. Nobody could block Wally Goodwin's jump shot. Nobody."

Imagine Sam's surprise, then, when his team of New York City high-school basketball all-stars—among them, Goodwin—took on a bunch from Washington, D.C., in a New Jersey tournament one enlightening day in 1962.

"I'd never heard of Dave Bing," admitted Penceal. "The name meant nothing to me. But then we started to play, and Wally went up for a shot...and Bing blocked it. He blocked Wally Goodwin's jumper! And I was, like, 'Wow. This is amazing. This cat, Bing, can really get up.' Then, I saw the rest of his game and realized he could do everything. That was my first encounter with Dave Bing."

Penceal would experience others because he and Bing would both enroll at Syracuse in the fall—Sam, from Boys High School in Brooklyn; Dave from Spingarn High in D.C. And they'd both play three years of varsity ball for the Orangemen. Only one of them, though, would become the indelible face of a majestic program.

"Even after all these years," Penceal said, "from what I've seen, Dave Bing is still the best player to ever play at Syracuse. No doubt."

Well, of course. Bing—who chose to attend SU, in part, because he was unsure how effective he could be at UCLA, Michigan and those other powerhouses that had recruited him—led the Syracuse club in scoring in each of his three seasons (22.2, 23.2 and 28.4) and in rebounding twice (12.0 and 10.8). And while assists did not make for an official statistic back then between 1963-64 and 1965-66, you can safely assume that the six-foot-three Bing had more of those than any of his Orange teammates, too.

"But you want to know something?" Penceal asked. "What really impressed me about Dave was what he was like off the floor. He was just a regular guy. Even when he became a superstar pro and a successful businessman, he remained just a regular guy. And he was always looking to help other people."

Bing certainly helped Chuck Richards, who wasn't sure if he wanted to transfer to Syracuse from the U.S. Military Academy, during a weekend visit in 1962. And he did so simply by playing in a few pickup games at Archbold Gymnasium with Richards, a six-foot-nine center whose eyes became saucers.

"So, there I am, out on the floor with the guy," said Richards, who'd been raised in Poland, N.Y. "I was from rural New York. I'd never been on a court with a player like him, but it only took three or four times up and down the floor to realize what Dave Bing was all about. He found me with these great passes under the basket each time. By the time we were through I was thinking, 'Whoa, I want to play with this guy.' And that was only the beginning."

Of a beautiful relationship, that is. Indeed, in the history of Syracuse basketball, there has been only one season in which two different Orangemen averaged 20 points or more per game. And that was in 1963-64 when Bing and Richards formed a wondrous one-two punch.

"It was my junior year (22.0 ppg) and his sophomore year (22.2 ppg)," said Richards. "But Dave probably gave me 16 of my points on easy layups. He could have easily averaged 35 a game. I'm telling you, the guy was Oscar Robertson. He would routinely get 25 points, 11 assists and 10 rebounds a game. And the thing is, Dave was as tremendous a person as he was a player."

As a player, Bing averaged 24.8 points and 10.3 rebounds per game during his career at Syracuse and was so spectacular as a Piston, Bullet and Celtic that he was named to the NBA's 50th Anniversary All-Time Team in 1996. As a person, meanwhile, he evolved into both a noted philanthropist and business giant in the Detroit area where he runs the remarkable Bing Group, a collection of manufacturing companies that produces parts for the automotive, appliance and office furniture industries.

He wasn't bad as a safety net, either.

"Whenever we went out, we made sure we had Dave with us," said Dick Ableman, who played with Bing at SU for three years. "That way, if we got into any trouble, we knew we'd be all right. If Freddie Lewis was going to hand out some discipline—you know, bench people or something—he'd have to figure out something else and go easy on us. Because there was no way that he was ever going to play a game without Dave Bing in the lineup."

After all, a Wally Goodwin kind of character might have been on the other side. And somebody would have been needed to block his jumper.

SAM, YOU'VE GOT BARRY AND BRADLEY

He was only a sophomore at the time, a kid out of Brooklyn's Boys High School in his first varsity season with just six college games under his belt. But, ready or not, there was Sam Penceal, plopped down amid some serious sneakered greatness.

The Orangemen were in Miami, Florida., for the Hurricane Classic in December of 1963, and joining them there were the Miami Hurricanes, Princeton Tigers and Army Black Knights. Which means that with the exception of the Army club, Penceal could not have swung a bag of dirty laundry without hitting a future legend in the chops.

The Father-Son-and-Holy Ghost list of guys in the building who would ultimately play 36 seasons of professional basketball? They were:

—Rick Barry, who was a junior at Miami and in the process of averaging 29.8 points and 16.5 rebounds during his Hurricanes career.

—Bill Bradley, who was a junior at Princeton and in the process of averaging 30.1 points and 12.1 rebounds during his Tigers career.

—Dave Bing, who was a sophomore at SU and in the process of averaging 24.8 points and 10.3 rebounds during his Orange career.

That's 6,684 combined college points and 3,068 combined college rebounds in 236 combined college games for an average of 28.3 points and 13.0 rebounds per game per "B"—Barry, Bradley and Bing. And all of that talent was on display for two glorious evenings in Miami's Convention Hall.

Penceal's role? The good part was that he started with Bing for the Orangemen, which proved to be an unquestioned privilege. The bad part, though, was that Sam's primary responsibility was to guard both the six-foot-seven Barry and the six-foot-five Bradley—a daunting challenge for a lot of reasons, not the least of which was the fact that he stood merely six-foot-two.

But as SU won that '63 Hurricane Classic with its conquests of Princeton (76-71) and Miami (86-85, in OT), you can assume that Sam—who'd later dedicate 30 years of his adulthood to high-school and college education in New York and Cleveland—did a pretty good job.

"Barry was perhaps the most difficult guy I ever played against because he was so agile," Penceal said. "But he was sick for that game. He had a fever. I mean, he never even warmed up. I remember seeing Rick just sitting over there on the bench, wrapped in towels and shivering. And then, all during the warmups before the second half, he did the same thing all over again. He just sat there in his sweats, bundled up in towels. But to tell you the truth, when he was on the floor, none of it seemed to bother him too much."

Apparently not, because Barry, sick as he was, still managed to drop 25 points on Penceal and the Orangemen that night.

The previous evening, however, had been a different story, because it was then that Penceal and the other Syracuse defenders held Bradley to the lowest offensive production of his college career—17 points, on seven-of-11 accuracy from the field (plus three free throws). To be fair, though, you should know that Bradley did foul out with 12:49 to play in the second half.

"Oh, man, he was a tremendous shooter, let me tell you," Penceal said. "And another thing: You know how everybody says how Tim Duncan (of the NBA's San Antonio Spurs) is so fundamentally sound? Well, Bradley was exactly the same kind of player.

"And he got his revenge the next year. We played Princeton at the Holiday Festival, and Bill scored 36 points on me. And they beat us, too. I had all my friends and family there at Madison Square Garden and he put 36 on me. Nobody who was at that game has ever let me forget it."

So, there. End of story. End of Sam Penceal's brushes with greatness during his sophomore-year trip to south Florida. Right?

Wrong.

"We had a trainer named Jules Reichel," said Penceal, "and he'd worked at the 1960 Olympics, and while he was there in Rome, he got to know Muhammad Ali. Well, Ali was in Miami at the time, training at the Fifth Street Gym for his first fight with Sonny Liston. So Jules took Bing and me to meet him. Of course, we thought that was great.

"Ali was going to take us around in his big red convertible, but we had to get back to practice. So, instead, he came to the Princeton game to watch us play. He came in with his whole retinue and sat in the first row and talked to us the whole time. If I remember correctly, Fred Lewis, our coach, wasn't too happy that we were having a running conversation with Muhammad Ali during the course of the game. But we did, anyway."

Hmm. Rick Barry... Bill Bradley... Dave Bing... Muhammad Ali, who was then known as Cassius Clay. Certainly, young Sam Penceal had plenty about which to write to the folks on the backs of his Florida postcards.

A REBOUNDING MAN

If you've been in the New York City area since 1976, and have flipped your radio dial to WBLS (107.5 FM) Mondays through Fridays between 10 p.m.-2 a.m., you've likely heard the mellow voice of the host of "The Quiet Storm." Imagine a comfy sweater or a cushy sofa or a favored glass of sherry. Do that, and you're listening to Vaughn Harper.

"I've had this voice since I was in college," Harper said. "The guys on the team didn't take note of it, but the ladies did."

That "college" was Syracuse University and those "guys on the team" were the basketball Orangemen of the mid-to-late 1960s. And the "ladies" in question? Sure, they might have been SU coeds spellbound by Harper's melodious pipes. But then, maybe they were simply attracted by the sight of a rebounding man.

And Vaughn Harper—now a cool-cooler-coolest disc jockey for more than a quarter-century, but then anything but a "quiet" storm on the boards—was a rebounding man.

"I loved to rebound," said Harper, who came to Syracuse from Boys High School in Brooklyn. "It was my thing. It came natural to me. You know how people used to talk about how Dennis Rodman could rebound? Well, that's how I rebounded. All out. All the time."

In the history of SU basketball—and that's a history that predates the flight of the Wright Brothers—only nine Orangemen have grabbed more rebounds than Harper. Importantly, five of them played four seasons and all of them stood at least six-foot-seven.

Harper? The rules said he could not participate as a freshman, so he was restricted to just 79 games spread across three campaigns—1965-66 through 1967-68. Oh, and he was only six-foot-four.

"I played every position," said Harper, whose 11.1 career per-game rebounding average has been bettered by only three Syracuse athletes—six-foot-seven Jon Cincebox (14.6), six-foot-11 Bill Smith (12.9) and six-foot-eight Rudy Hackett (11.4). "I used to jump center. I mean, I had to. Other than me, we didn't have anybody who could jump. You know, except for Dave Bing."

Imagine this: Though Bing was six-foot-three and Harper was six-foot-four, one or the other led SU in rebounding during a stretch of four consecutive years—Bing in 1964-65 (12.0) and 1965-66 (10.8); Harper in 1966-67 (14.3) and 1967-68 (10.9). Why, Bing pulled down 25 rebounds in a 1966 affair with Cornell and Harper grabbed 23 in a 1967 contest against Colgate.

So, despite their size, they could go get them. And the NBA's Detroit franchise noticed because the Pistons selected Bing and Harper in the '66 and '67 drafts, respectively. Only Bing, however, stuck.

Make no mistake, though, that Harper—also a 1,000-point scorer who averaged 13.5 points during his Orange career—could play. And he proved it conclusively during the 1966 Quaker City Classic at the Palestra in Philadelphia, Pa., where he won the MVP trophy even though SU lost to No. 2-ranked Louisville on the second of the eight-team tournament's three evenings of competition.

"Louisville had Wes Unseld and Butch Beard, and I played them to death," said Harper, the so-called 'Kangaroo Kid' who scored 24 points, grabbed 18 rebounds and passed off for three assists against the Cardinals. "My whole career happened that night.

"I remember Fred Lewis telling Dave Aldrich, 'When Unseld goes to rebound, you stand there and face him. Wherever he goes, you go. Got that?' And then he told me, 'And you, Harper. You go get the rebounds.' And that's what we did. We lost (75-71). But we should have won, to be honest with you. Butch Beard tells me that to this day."

His voice wasn't an angry one as he spoke; rather, it softly rumbled in the fashion of a...yeah, a quiet storm. All these years later, Vaughn Harper, the big-city disc jockey, still sounded good. Probably could still rebound, too.

JIM BOEHEIM'S BAD BODY

It took some doing, but Mother Nature finally kicked in for Jim Boeheim, who was nothing if not the picture of 58-year-old nattiness down in New Orleans where his Orangemen won the 2003 national championship by surviving both Texas and Kansas at the Final Four.

Truth be told, with his fetching wardrobe, fancy spectacles and fashionable haircut, Boeheim, the long-time (and filled-out) Syracuse coach, has been a fairly dashing figure for a while now. However, once upon a time—or back when the man resembled a 7-iron with ears—such was not the case.

"I remember the first time I saw Jimmy," said Chuck Richards, a one-time FBI agent who played varsity ball for two SU seasons with Boeheim. "It was 1962, and he was a freshman. And he staggered out to practice, with his glasses on, at about six-foot-four and 135 pounds. I couldn't believe what I was seeing. He didn't look like he could play in the local 'Y' league."

It turned out that Boeheim's scarecrow looks were deceiving because he ended up playing well enough to average 9.8 points (on 52 percent shooting from the floor), 2.4 assists and 2.3 rebounds—not to mention a whole bunch of floor burns—in his 76 games as an Orangeman. Further, he had enough talent in the tank to very nearly make the Chicago Bulls roster after having graduated from Syracuse in 1966.

But the truth of the matter is, the youthful Jim Boeheim—the son of a mortician who looked like the son of a mortician—could have passed for Olive Oyl's twin brother.

"If you bumped into Jimmy, he'd fold up like a wet sack of month-old bananas," said Rick Dean, who is now a Methodist minister but for two years was one of Boeheim's Orange teammates. "He was a nerd before nerds were nerds. He was always wearing those thick glasses, and he was always pushing them up on his nose, trying to see what was going on.

"He couldn't run. He couldn't jump. He couldn't see. He was the weakest, spaghetti-legged ballplayer I ever came across. If we'd had a weight-training program back then, Jimmy wouldn't have been able to lift the bar with nothing on it. But guess what? Nobody could run him out of the lineup. He had as good a court sense as any person I've ever seen. And he could shoot. If you left him to cheat on Dave Bing, Jimmy would bury it on you. He did it all the time."

Believe it or not, Boeheim would do that jump-shooting thing with panache...with an undeniable *duende*...with a certain *je ne sais quoi*. Or maybe not.

"Jim was the original floppy-socks guy; not Pete Maravich," said Sam Penceal, a long-time educator who came to Syracuse with Boeheim in '62 and left with him in '66. "But he wasn't styling. Uh uh. Boeheim's legs were so skinny, his socks were always falling down on him. And it wasn't something he was particularly happy about.

"We used to call him 'Farmer.' And he wasn't too happy about that, either. But he was from Lyons, N.Y., which is farm country. You know, he sort of looked like a farmer and he didn't have the suaveness that we city boys had—or thought we had—so we'd tease him. I remember after Jim became a big-time coach, I called him 'Farmer' and he gave me one of those looks that said, 'Don't call me "Farmer" any more.'"

Well, it did beat "Spaghetti Legs."

DON'T MATCH RESUMES WITH THIS MAN

There have been all kinds of fascinating folks who've played basketball for the Orangemen since their school's first game in 1901. Why, so vast is their number that to dare anoint one above all the others is to traffic in folly.

Nevertheless, a good case could be made for Rick Dean, whose life suggests that he should have been twins. At least.

He came to Syracuse from Cherry Hill, N.J., and started under Fred Lewis for three years from 1964-65 through 1966-67, during which time the Orangemen went 55-22 and were once ranked as high as No. 7 in the land. So, Dean could play—well enough, in fact, to ultimately be drafted by both the NBA and the dearly departed ABA. And at six-foot-six and 230 pounds, he could clean up Dodge, too.

"I was a very physical, hard-nosed kind of guy," said Dean, who averaged 18.0 points and 9.1 rebounds per game as a senior. "I've gotta tell you, I enjoyed banging people around and knocking them down."

But he was so much more than an athletic strongboy. Indeed, upon graduation from SU in 1967, Dean listened to Dave Bing—who was then the NBA's newly crowned Rookie of the Year—advise him that he could play in the league...and he stunningly chose, instead, to (1) enlist in the U.S. Army, and (2) volunteer for infantry duty in Vietnam.

Thereafter, Dean joined the FBI (just like his father) and stayed with it for three years. And then he taught and coached and administrated on the high-school level for a couple of decades. And then, in the early 1990s, he went to seminary and became a minister, eventually landing at Higgins Memorial United Methodist Church in Burnsville, N.C.

So, there. Professional-caliber athlete (and second-team Academic All-American), war-time soldier, second-generation FBI agent, teacher/coach/administrator, Methodist minister, husband, and father. How many people on your block have a resume that stands up to that?

More remarkable yet, how many have a silver star, a bronze star and an Army commendation medal, all of which were earned at the hellish mouth of Vietnam's Au Shau Valley, a 22-mile stretch along the DMZ that was the turf of thousands of Viet Cong?

"I was an infantry platoon leader," said Dean, then a member of the 101st Airborne Division. "I was carrying a rifle in the rice paddies, shooting people almost every day. In combat action my company commander was wounded, one of the other lieutenants was killed and another one was wounded. So, I took over command of the company, finished the firefight and evacuated the wounded and the dead. And the Army called me a hero."

He was 22 then. Maybe 23. And all these years later, Rick Dean, who came home a captain, can't forget. Won't forget, either.

"I would say that the trust this country put in me, as an officer, to lead other young men in combat is probably the highest honor I've ever had," he declared. "You know, you always have regrets. Could I have made it in the NBA? Well, Dave Bing thought I could, and that's a pretty good recommendation. But the way I look at it, if the idea is to learn about life—and the choice is between professional basketball or leading men in combat—I chose the right way."

Jump shots, after all, go only so far.

CHASING THOSE 100 POINTS

They were scoring fools during the 1965-66 season. Absolute scoring fools. How so? The Orangemen scored 98 points against Vanderbilt...and lost by 15. They yielded 105 points to Colgate...and won by 20. In their first 10 games, they scored 1,027 points. In a five-game stretch during the middle of the campaign, they scored 552 points. In their last five games prior to the NCAA Tournament, they scored 508 points.

They scored and scored and scored, that's what Fred Lewis's Orangemen did when Dave Bing was a senior and averaging 28.4 points a night against all comers. They wore out statisticians' pencils from Manley Field House all the way to Los Angeles and back again. And as they heaved from near and far, they came within one lousy field goal of making history.

"If we could have scored 124 points on that last night," recalled Rick Dean, "we would have been the first team in NCAA history to average 100 points per game in the regular season."

Alas, the SU boys could manage "only" 122 on the evening of March 5, 1966, finishing with 2,598 points in 26 contests for an average of 99.92 per game. Oh, but they gave it a run once the Colgate Red Raiders—who'd been whomped by Syracuse, 125-105, 19 days earlier—had marched into manic Manley and, upon arrival, were all but given blindfolds.

"We knew beforehand that we needed 124 points, and to be honest with you we didn't care about the final score," said Dean, who was then a meaty six-foot-six, 230-pound junior averaging 12.1 points and 5.2 rebounds per game. "We knew we were going to beat Colgate. We were better than they were. We just wanted those 124 points, and if that meant letting them shoot so we could get the ball back and shoot it ourselves, fine."

Make no mistake that they chucked it often—98 times from the field, as a matter of fact (draining 48 of the attempts)—while the largest-ever Manley crowd (at the time) of 7,105 howled, and howled some more. Bing went for 31 and Dean went for 17 and Jim Boeheim went for 17 and Vaughn Harper went for 14 and George Hicker went for 14 and six other Orangemen combined for 29 more.

"The goal of that game," said Dean, "was: 'If you get the ball, shoot it.' We were committing fouls just to let them take free throws, so we could get the ball back. I remember at the end, one of us had the ball and he missed the shot and they got the rebound, and then we tried to steal it and we missed that, too. And then, they ran out the clock and the game was over."

The final was 122-88, and it marked the 14th time that those 1965-66 Orangemen—who would finish with a final won-lost record of 22-6—had scored at least 100 points in a contest. And none of it was by accident.

"Basically, everybody on that team had the green light to shoot, as long as the shot was in your range," said Dean, who would become a ninth-round draft choice of the then-San Francisco Warriors. "Our strategy was simple: Shoot the ball, and then go to the boards. And if the ball went in the basket, we'd flop right into our full-court press. And we'd stay in that full-court press for 40 minutes, no matter what the score was."

Dean, who was destined to become both an honorable mention All-American and a second-team Academic All-American as a senior, was a happy beneficiary of all of this. In fact, during SU's first date with the Red Raiders that season—the aforementioned 125-105 monstrosity in Hamilton, N.Y.—he was pretty much the Orange version of Don Larsen, the old New York Yeankees pitcher.

"We were at Colgate and we were sitting in the locker room at halftime, and Lewis was looking over the stat sheet," said Dean of the thing that showed Syracuse holding a massive 74-49 lead. "And he announces, 'Rick, you're 10-for-10 from the field. You've got a perfect game going.' When they heard that, the guys started telling me they were going to pass me the ball in the second half until I missed. I said, 'You can feed me all you want. I'm not shooting.'

"Seriously, I remember being very ginger in the second half. The three shots I made were all layups, so I ended up 13-for-13, which tied the NCAA record at the time. I think it's up to 16-for-16 now. But I missed a free throw. I was four-for-five at the line, so that was the fly in the ointment."

Ah, but what a nice ointment it was, because Dean bagged 30 points against the Red Raiders that night at Huntington Gym and helped those Orangemen, scoring fools that they were, along the path that nearly wended its way into the offensive history books and to the Final Four.

But...no. You see, in the finals of the East Regional that year, the Orangemen could manage but 81 points—what a shame, huh?—against Duke, and lost by seven. That game, though, was played on the second of back-to-back days. Which means those Blue Devils might have been in some serious trouble if Syracuse had been allowed to catch its breath. Catch its breath, that is, and take aim.

LEARNING A ROLE

He was a six-foot-five center who'd averaged some 33 points a game as a senior during the 1965-66 season at tiny Milford High School, just outside Oneonta, N.Y. And even though he weighed, oh, 165 pounds with ball bearings in his pockets, Mike Barlow—a member of a graduating class of 40—was going to be a star at Syracuse University.

Or at least he was going to get a lot of playing time for the Orangemen. Or so he thought.

"I ended up being just a journeyman," Barlow said. "I used to ask, 'How come I'm not playing?' Well, when I look back now, I know why. I wasn't a true big man and I wasn't quick enough to play outside. I didn't know it then, but I know it now."

He did have an inkling, though. And it was supported by the stat sheet, which showed Barlow getting into just nine games as a sophomore and only seven games as a junior before a bout with hepatitis limited him to a mere three games as a senior. So he turned his attention to another sport. To baseball, which Syracuse used to play until the school disbanded the program following the 1972 season.

Frankly, it was a wise decision, because after signing with the Oakland Athletics out of SU in 1970 and being shipped off to Coos Bay, Oregon, where he made the princely sum of $500 a month as a right-handed pitcher, Barlow steadily worked his way through the minors and landed with the St. Louis Cardinals in 1975.

He eventually migrated to the Houston Astros, California Angels and Toronto Blue Jays, staying in the big leagues for seven seasons, during which he went 10-6 with six saves and a 4.63 earned run average in 133 games. Importantly, Barlow pitched for the Angels in the 1979 American League Championship Series against Baltimore.

So, he was good. Real good. And one of the reasons Barlow was good—one of the reasons why he'd succeeded as a lanky pitcher—was because he had failed, comparatively speaking, as a skinny center.

"I played for Fred Lewis," said Barlow, who is the athletic director at Bishop Grimes High School in East Syracuse, N.Y. "He's the guy who recruited me out of Milford. And I remember him taking some of us aside one day and saying, 'Fellas, you're still Division I players. No matter what your role is on this team, you're still part of an elite group of guys to be able to play on the Division I level.'

"I found out at Syracuse that some pretty good athletes ride the bench. And that helped me move up in professional baseball, because I was taught by Lewis how to accept a role. You know, you come out of high school and you're a star. But when you put all the stars together, suddenly not everybody is a star anymore. So, you end up on the bench and you learn that your job is to be ready when you get called."

To be ready when you get called, huh? Isn't that the creed of the relief pitcher? And isn't it interesting that Mike Barlow started twice, and only twice, in those 133 games he played in the big leagues?

Coincidence? Think again.

THE ITALIAN LEPRECHAUN
AND THE DOVES

He was—along with SU's Jim Boeheim, Georgetown's John Thompson and Villanova's Rollie Massimino—one of the Big East Conference's godfathers, one of its Four Musketeers, one of its coaching Beatles. And almost nobody in Orange Nation didn't like him.

Oh, his voice sounded as if he'd gargled with carpenter tacks, his sweater often looked as if it had been pulled off the back of a horse, and he wasn't above giving an earful to a passing referee. But Lou Carnesecca, the Italian leprechaun who danced along the St. John's sideline in 24 seasons during a 27-year stretch, was as embraced in Syracuse as any bad guy could ever hope to be.

"Sure, I was beloved there," he rasped, "because the Orangemen always beat me. Every time I walked in the place—Manley Field House, the Dome...it didn't matter— I'd get a big hand. You know, it was like, 'Thanks for coming. Glad to see ya.' I lost to Syracuse so often, they should have held a few benefits for me.

"I mean, it was tough winning up there. Take Manley Field House. Holy mackerel. I'm a little bit deaf now, but I wish I was deaf back then. Those fans were right on top of you, and they'd let you have it from all angles. They had a way of expressing themselves, let me tell you. And then they moved into the Dome and it was like playing in an airport hangar. No wonder I hardly ever won up there."

Truth is, Carnesecca's clubs nearly broke even with the Orangemen as they went 19-21 between 1965-92 against SU outfits coached by Fred Lewis, Roy Danforth and Boeheim. But Looie won just four of his last 13 games against Boeheim, so we can forgive him his melodrama.

The point is, Carnesecca did win his share through the years. One of the more memorable of those triumphs took place on February 21, 1967, when St. John's came into Manley to take on eighth-ranked SU—19-2 at the time, and a winner of 12 in a row (and 22 straight at home)—and knocked off the Orangemen, 71-64.

"Oh, that," said Carnesecca, who retired in 1992, the very year he was inducted into the Naismith Basketball Hall of Fame in Springfield, Massachusetts, with a 526-200 record at St. John's. "That was the famous Sonny Dove game."

Dove, you may recall, was the Redmen's terrific All-America forward whose three-year career averages were 19.0 points and 12.5 rebounds per game. And he was so revered by the St. John's followers that they periodically hailed him in a most unique way. And they did so again that night in Manley, where 6,473 roarers had gathered amid the dust and tumult.

"Our fans wanted to give us an emotional lift, so some of them released doves inside the building," said Carnesecca, who watched Dove, the six-foot-eight human, torch the Orangemen for 27 points and 12 rebounds that magical evening. "I'm talking real, live birds. Three or four of them. You know, in honor of Sonny, who was a senior. It was unbelievable. They flew around the place during the game and the crowd went crazy.

"It wasn't exactly like Red Auerbach lighting up a victory cigar, but it was along those lines. The people loved it. They reacted. It was like, 'Wow. Look at those birds.' I'll bet some of them are still up there in the rafters. Or if not them, at least their sons and daughters."

The Big East's coaching Beatles—Boeheim, Thompson, Massimino and Carnesecca—have long since broken up. And as they worked, through Boeheim's 2002-03 SU campaign, for a total of 97 seasons at Syracuse, Georgetown, Villanova and St. John's, respectively, there is some melancholy in that.

They're all still around, though, which is the good news. But only one of them thinks of Manley Field House and talks about the sons and daughters of birds. That would be the Italian leprechaun, who has forever kept folks (even Syracuse folks) smiling.

SU's Blackout Season

George Hicker, who grew up an hour south of Buffalo, N.Y., and wowed 'em with his jump shot in Syracuse, had himself a dandy 2003. He's a Los Angeles-area guy now, having made a fair amount of money in Southern California's industrial real-estate game. But he's forever been a sports fan...and, oh, he had a year.

The Anaheim Angels began the baseball season as the defending World Series champions. The Anaheim Mighty Ducks played their way into the Stanley Cup Finals. And his Orangemen knocked off six consecutive opponents— including four from the Big 12 Conference—in the NCAA Tournament to win the national championship.

Strangely, though, all of that success inspired George to reflect on his final painful days in Syracuse under the rule of Fred Lewis.

"It's funny about teams," he said. "The Angels. The Mighty Ducks. The Orangemen. No one was thinking about them. I mean, Syracuse wasn't even in anybody's preseason Top 25 for the first time in I don't know how long. But it didn't matter. Look what they did.

"And then there was our team, my senior year. I believe in one poll, we were picked No. 3 in the country at the beginning of the season. And then we finished 11-14. So, you never know what's going to happen."

That campaign—the 1967-68 edition, featuring one foul stretch during which SU lost seven in a row, 11 of 13, and 13 of 15—proved to be the last of Lewis's six seasons at the head of the Orange bench. And it was a bad one. As bad as five miles of gravel road.

"We had a bunch of suspensions, and things happened between the players and Fred," said Hicker, who'd led Syracuse in scoring as a junior with his 18.6 average. "We had guys like Ernie Austin and Wayne Ward, who were potential All-American types. But we just never jelled. It just goes to show that something can be something on paper, but how it ends up can have nothing to do with what's on paper. If you know what I mean."

Now, you must understand that George Hicker was some kind of player. He scored 1,245 points during his three-year career and has to make anybody's short list of the greatest shooters ever to wear an SU uniform. And in his adulthood, he did become fast friends with Lewis, who'd left Syracuse in 1968 to become the athletic director at Sacramento State.

But the relationship between the wonderful athlete and the steel-belted coach ruptured under the strain of all those losses during that last long winter.

"There was a lot of bitterness when I left school," admitted Hicker. "By then, Lewis and I weren't even speaking. He suspended me for one game because of what happened the night Calvin Murphy went for 65 (actually, 50) against us at Manley Field House.

"He took me out at some point and said, 'You're not playing anymore unless you start playing some defense.' And I said, 'I am playing defense.' And he said, 'You're done. Go to the locker room.' And I didn't. I sat at the end of the bench and all kinds of things happened after that. And he suspended me for the next game."

Well, the Orangemen lost that evening—January 31, 1968—to Murphy's Niagara Purple Eagles, 116-107. And, without Hicker, they lost three nights later to Bobby Knight's Army club by 20 points. And they finished with a losing record just a year after having gone 20-6, and just two years after having nearly made it to the Final Four.

And it was...sad. Hicker, after all, had spurned the likes of Notre Dame and Iowa and dozens and dozens of other schools to sign on with Syracuse. And he'd done so because of Fred Lewis. And also because of Fred Lewis's gem.

"I went there for a weekend visit," recalled Hicker, a six-foot-three forward from little Franklinville, N.Y. "And I went into the gym...and there was Dave Bing. Let me tell you, once you walk into a gym with Dave Bing in it, you forget about everybody else who might be in there. I looked at him and said to myself, 'That's it. I'm coming to school here.' And I did."

George played his sophomore year with Bing and Jim Boeheim and the rest of that wild bunch, which attempted an every-game assault on 100 points. And then, as a junior, he flowered into a star himself. But during his senior season, the whole thing splattered like an egg having rolled off a counter top and onto the kitchen floor...and Hicker and Lewis went their separate ways.

"I've kind of blacked a lot of it out," Hicker said. "But Fred and I both grew up a little bit and we definitely became friends. In fact, there were only a few of us who kept up with him right to the end when he died. And I was one of them. It might have ended badly, but you have to wonder if Syracuse basketball would have gotten to the point it has without Fred Lewis. He brought in Bing and Sam Penceal and Vaughn Harper. He's the one who started it all. And look where it is now."

To do so—to look where Orange hoops is now—you'd have to tilt your head. Up. Way, way up. Even all the way out there in Southern California.

UH-HUH, IT WAS THE FRED LEWIS

So, there was Joe Hamelin sitting in his northern California office at the *Sacramento Bee,* and the telephone was ringing. And so Joe picked it up and heard a most inquisitive voice.

"You wrote in your column this morning something about Clair Bee spinning in his grave," the voice said. "But I think he's still alive. Do you know, in fact, that he's dead? I played for him and this is news to me."

"Oh, come on," said Joe. "The man would have to be 106 if he was still alive, but I'm more than willing to concede that I haven't checked out his tombstone. If I've made a mistake, I'd be happy to correct it. By the way, who am I talking to?"

"My name," the voice said, "is Fred Lewis."

And Hamelin, who'd worked as a newspaperman for a while in Utica, N.Y., when a fellow by that name had coached the Syracuse University basketball team, sat up straight in his chair.

"Are you," Joe asked, "*the* Fred Lewis?"

"Nobody," the voice replied after a pause, "has called me *the* Fred Lewis for a long, long time."

Well, it was him. It was *the* Fred Lewis, the one who'd rescued the Orangemen, losers of 27 of their previous 29 games, after stepping onto the SU campus in 1962 as Marc Guley's replacement. It was *the* Fred Lewis, the one who'd imported Dave Bing and Jim Boeheim and Vaughn Harper and Chuck Richards and Sam Penceal and George Hicker and Rick Dean and a whole lot of others, and ordered them to run foes until those foes became puddles. It was *the* Fred Lewis, the one who'd taken over a listing 2-22 program and 46 games later had it ranked No. 7 in the nation.

Yeah, it was *the* Fred Lewis, all right. Not that anybody out there in Sacramento much noticed.

"By then," remembered Hamelin, "Fred was a teacher living in a town where basically nobody knew who the hell he was."

Tired of his $13,000 annual salary, weary of seeing Ben Schwartzwalder's football team being granted its every wish while the basketball players begged for socks, and eager to put his doctorate to better use, Lewis bolted from Syracuse in 1968 to become the athletic director at Sacramento State University in a failed attempt to move up the food chain.

Never mind that the Orangemen went from 2-22 in 1961-62 under Guley to 17-8 in 1963-64 under Lewis. Never mind that SU averaged 99.0 points per game in 1965-66 (without any silly three-point line, either) and very nearly qualified for the Final Four. Never mind that Syracuse had one glorious stretch of 57-15 and that it had turned Manley Field House into a passion pit.

No, never mind all of that. After six seasons of basketball resurrection, Fred Lewis, who'd come to town after a coaching gig at Southern Mississippi, was gone. And not too long after that—just a few years, really, following too many clashes with those around him—he was gone, too, from the AD's chair at Sacramento State. As such, he became a professor and stayed in the classroom until his retirement. He remained in California until he passed away from cancer at the age of 73 in 1994.

Before dying, though, he'd evolved into a dear, dear friend to Hamelin, whose column had inspired that inquisitive telephone call. And each and every Tuesday, for 10 straight years following that telephone call, the two men— one of whom had never much cared for sportswriters— would clear their calendars and sit down for lunch. And, sure, the salt-and-pepper shakers and the condiment bottles were regularly moved around the table.

This one would be Bing...that one was Boeheim...over there were Harper and Hicker and Dean.

"Fred was an innovator, a motivator," said Hamelin of his pal who'd gone 91-57 at SU. "He used to tell me how they pressed and ran the whole game. I mean, from beginning to end. Nobody had done that. Not from the jump ball to the final horn. But his teams did."

Heck, in the 1965-66 season, alone, the Orangemen had contests during which they scored 125, 122, 120, 118, 114 (twice), 113, 110, 106, 105, 103 (twice), and 100 (twice) points. And, yeah, along the way they'd periodically anger guys on the receiving end—not that Lewis much cared. And why would he? He'd been a Marine and had lost some hearing when a land mine exploded and blew out his right ear drum. He'd played pro ball for the old Sheboygan Redskins, Birmingham Skyhawks, Indianapolis Jets, and Baltimore Bullets. He'd shot a hole in his right hand during a hunting accident, a mishap that cost him the feel on his jump shot and ultimately ended his career.

He was, in other words, as tough as the fender on a bus. And this tough fellow didn't spend much time worrying about the cranky musings of others, some of whom, quite frankly, turned out to be his own players who'd found Lewis to be more ornery than he needed to be and not quite the bench coach his record suggested he was.

But then, Fred Lewis never did forget his time with the Orangemen, even if he wasn't ever invited, perhaps tellingly, by SU officials to step foot inside the Carrier Dome and take a bow. And when he reminisced, he mostly brightened.

"Oh, he loved Syracuse," Hamelin said. "He loved the university. And he was always so proud of Jim Boeheim.

Fred would talk about Boeheim all the time. And I loved listening. Every time we'd get together, I was sitting in a pear tree. You know something? I still miss him virtually every day. I'm telling you, he was the smartest man I've ever known. And he was the nicest man I've ever known. To me, he was 10 feet tall."

He was also correct, too, about Clair Bee, his old coach at Long Island University for whom Lewis—a guard with a whiz-bang jump shot—was the second-leading scorer in the nation during the 1944-45 season.

"Yeah, I'll admit it," Hamelin said. "Clair Bee was alive when I wrote that column. It was—ahem—one of the only mistakes I've made in my career."

But it was a good mistake. Because without it, Joe never would have met *the* Fred Lewis.

HE HELPED HOLD CALVIN
MURPHY TO 68 POINTS

It's not blaspheming if it's the truth, and Bob Kouwe swears it's the truth.

"When I was on the freshman team and Dave Bing was a senior, I'd take 30-second showers so I could get out of there and watch him play," said Kouwe. "That's how great I think Bing was. But as great as he was, and I guarded him a lot in practice so I know Dave Bing was absolutely great, watching him play was nothing—I mean, nothing—compared to watching Calvin Murphy play."

Well, Kouwe could be considered a font of knowledge on the subject, because in his last couple of years on the Syracuse varsity, the Orangemen played Murphy's Niagara Purple Eagles on two occasions. And in those two games, Murphy scored 118 points. Or a mere 59 per.

"And remember," said Kouwe, speaking in early retirement from his home in Tampa, Florida. "There was no three-point line back then. Think about that."

And now think about this: In the second of those two affairs—on December 7, 1968—Murphy went for 68 points in Niagara's 118-110 win at home. Sixty-eight points.

"We had Ernie Austin guard him," said Kouwe, a native of Newark, N.Y., who was then a senior starter. "We had John Suder guard him. We had Ray Balukas guard him. I guarded him. But there was no way. None. He was the fastest human being you've ever seen. He could run faster dribbling than anybody else could run without a ball, and he never mis-dribbled. So how do you cover that?

"We picked him up as soon as he crossed center court. We tried a box-and-one. We double-teamed him. We triple-teamed him. We'd play defense on him when we had the ball on the offensive end, and I'm serious about that. But it was fruitless. There was no playing Calvin Murphy. It was a total loss even trying."

Murphy was five-foot-nine. Didn't matter. Murphy weighed 165 pounds. Didn't matter. Murphy was the Purple Eagles' first, second and third options on offense, so everybody knew exactly what he was going to do. Didn't matter. He took 46 shots from the field that night and splashed 24 of them. He attempted 23 shots from the foul line that night and buried 20 of them. And when the statisticians were finished with their addition, Murphy had his 68 points. Oh, and six assists and six rebounds, too.

"You know what we were?" asked Kouwe, who, at six-foot-three, had six inches on Murphy—not that it did him any good. "We were amazed. Me, especially. There were three or four times when I was all over him. I mean, he'd go up for a 25- or a 30-foot jumper and I'd be blanketing him, with a hand in his face. And he just jumped straight up into the air, as high as he needed to go, and let fly with the most beautiful floaters you can imagine. And he hit nothing but net. I thought I did a pretty good job on Calvin that night. I really did. And he went for 68."

Remarkably, Murphy's show—and not much was as electrifying as The Calvin Murphy Show—began even before he'd launched his first gorgeous jumper.

"I remember that they actually stopped pregame drills so Calvin could go through his baton-twirling exhibition," recalled Bill Smith, who was SU's sophomore center on The 68-Point Night. "We didn't have to watch, but we did. We couldn't help ourselves. So, you've got to picture this: Both teams, and the entire crowd, have stopped what they're doing and they're staring at Calvin Murphy while he's twirling a baton. We're standing there on the court and we're thinking, 'My God, look what this guy can do.' We were psyched out before the game even began."

Certainly, the Orangemen weren't the only folks Calvin Murphy wowed. He did, after all, average 48.9 points per game for the Niagara freshman team in 1966-67. And in his three varsity seasons, Murphy averaged 33.1 points per game on 28.1 shots per game. So, he pretty much shredded every defense he saw.

But only two Syracuse opponents have ever scored more than 41 points in a single contest against the Orange in a history that dates back to 1901...and Calvin Murphy—who went for 50 as a sophomore at Manley Field House on January 31, 1968, and for those 68 some 10 months later as a junior back home in front of 3,200 worshipers at the tiny Student Center at Niagara—is both of them.

"He could run," said Kouwe, whose nephew, Andrew, was a walk-on member of SU's 2003 national championship club. "He could dunk two-handed behind his head. He could shoot. And the fans would go absolutely wild. I mean, they were crazy for him. And you know something else? Calvin Murphy was the nicest guy in the world."

Why, Murphy was so nice that he sent a photo—taken on that 68-point evening, and then enlarged—to Kouwe's bachelor party in 1988. And he took the time to autograph it, too.

"*To Bob,*" it reads. "*Thanks for the memories. Calvin Murphy.*"

"I take flak over that picture, oh, 20 times a year," said Kouwe. "All my buddies are always on my butt about that. But it could have been worse because, like I told you, we didn't have the three-point line back then."

And if you'd had it, Bob was asked, how many points would Calvin Murphy have scored on the night he dropped 68 big ones atop the heads of those helpless Orangemen?

"Eighty," he said. "Easy. I kid you not. Eighty."

No blasphemy, just fact.

YO, THE NAME IS JO JO

To his players at Fairleigh Dickinson University, where he's run the basketball show since 1983, his name is Tom Green. Coach Tom Green. But to his old Syracuse teammates—especially those who were in Kansas's Allen Fieldhouse on December 14, 1968, for the Sunflower Doubleheader—he'll always be "Jo Jo."

Green was a sophomore then. A sophomore who would grow into (1) the Orangemen's starting point guard as a junior and senior, and (2) one of their assistant coaches for four seasons in the mid-'70s. But on that day, he was just a kid on an 0-4 SU team that was about to take the floor against the 11th-ranked Jayhawks and Jo Jo White, the All-America senior guard whose wondrous talent would ultimately inspire the Boston Celtics to retire his jersey number.

"I remember Roy Danforth's strategy going into that one," said Bill Smith, who was Syracuse's center back then. "He told us, 'The only chance we've got is if we win the opening tip, hold the ball, take the only shot at the end of the game and make it. Then, we'll win, 2-0.' As you can imagine, he was not instilling a lot of confidence in us."

The no-brainer idea for the winless Orangemen—who'd lost the day before by 20 to Kansas State—was to slow the ball down against once-beaten KU, which was averaging an even 80.0 points per contest. But that idea quickly went out the window and became just another tumbleweed on the prairie.

"We got into a running game with them, which was not the thing to do, and they pasted us," Smith said of the Jayhawks, who frolicked to a 71-41 victory. "But the really memorable thing was Tommy Green. He used to have this move where he'd be dribbling with his right hand and then do a reverse pivot and bring the ball behind him. You know, it was a spinaround kind of thing to get past a guy.

"Well, during the game, Tommy is bringing the ball down the court and Jo Jo White is guarding him...and Tommy tries to make that move. Big mistake. Because Jo Jo just reaches behind him, flicks the ball out, takes off downcourt and jams it mercilessly. After that, Tommy's move was referred to forevermore as the 'Jo Jo Whirl.' And Tommy got shortened up to 'Jo Jo.' Now, you know how Tommy Green got his nickname."

And so, too, do all those good Knights of Fairleigh Dickinson.

JIM BOEHEIM, GOLF COACH

Everybody knows everything about Jim Boeheim, the famous Syracuse basketball coach, by now. And why not? In his first 27 years guiding the Orangemen, he went 653-226 (.743), orchestrated 25 20-win seasons, won the 2003 national championship and guided his club to Final Fours in three successive decades—the '80s, the '90s, and the '00s.

But far too few people know about Jim Boeheim, the not-so-famous Syracuse golf coach.

Uh huh. One and the same.

"We were a ragged bunch," said Frank Beyer, who played on Boeheim's golf squad during the spring seasons of 1967, '68 and '69. "Other teams had uniforms and team bags and even team caddies. All we got from SU was two balls before each match. Well, one day Jim showed up at practice with team shirts. They were orange, with 'SU' on the front. I'm not sure the football team ever discovered who stole them."

Beyer, who graduated from SU in 1969 and is now the treasurer for Syracuse Utilities, Inc., recalls that his Orangemen were pretty much a .500 collection in those days. They'd win some matches; they'd lose some matches. But always they'd learn from their coach, who was in his early 20s, himself, and therefore only a few years older than any of them. And they'd learn about more than how to cure a slice.

"We drove to our matches all over the Northeast," said Beyer. "I was assigned to Boeheim's car, an Oldsmobile Cutlass convertible. My first year, I started out in the back seat behind Jim, and by the time I was a senior, I'd moved up to shotgun.

"I got lessons for three years during our travel days. Jim was exceptionally well-read, and there was a lot to discuss in the late '60s. I specifically remember talking about racial harmony and Jim thinking that a few generations of mixed marriages would help. He said, 'Diahann Carroll could be green and she'd still be a beautiful woman.'"

It's fairly common knowledge that Boeheim, who's played in Great Britain over more than a few summers, is quite the whiz-bang when it comes to the gentleman's game. In fact, after having won his share of College Basketball Coaches Invitational tournaments, he's generally considered by his peers to be the finest golfer among them. But that doesn't mean he hasn't experienced the periodic breakdown out there on the course.

"Boeheim was always a better player than most of us," Beyer said. "But he couldn't make short putts for money. We'd always have side bets in practice. At Penn State, he three-putted from four feet and lost a quarter. And he didn't talk to me for two days."

That may have beaten the alternative, because just as Boeheim has always picked on certain guys among his basketball players—think Rony Seikaly, Lukie Jackson, Kueth Duany, et al.—he did the same with his golfers, whom he coached in the late '60s and into the early '70s before the program was disbanded. And Beyer, poor Beyer, made for a nice target.

"We never had curfews," Beyer said. "We never had team rules. Jim felt that by the time you were old enough to go to college, you were old enough to behave yourself. But still, I was his whipping boy for three years. He used to get on my case over strategy in the matches where he questioned moves I made that he thought were mistakes. He usually got on me at the course while it was still fresh, but once we got in the car it was forgotten."

Boeheim's mind, though, was always working even if his mouth was at rest. Just like he's shown in basketball, he was forever thinking, tinkering, tweaking. And if he got a bit devious along the way? Well, the ends do justify the means, don't they?

"My senior year, I was undefeated betting in practice against my teammates, but I had a horrible record in matches," Beyer said. "I was 0-6 going into our match with Colgate, so Boeheim got the whole team to set up bets against me."

And Frank's response when he learned of his coach's dirty dealings?

"I closed out my guy on the 15th hole," he said, "going away."

THE (ALMOST) FORGOTTEN ORANGEMAN

If these were the good ol' days and "I've Got A Secret" was still on television, there is one former Orangeman who'd be sure to stump the panel.

A little theme music, please…

I hold Syracuse's all-time single-game scoring record with 47 points. I am one of only two SU players who played at least two varsity campaigns to have a career-scoring average in excess of 20 points per game (20.7). I own both the second-best career rebounds-per-game average (12.9) and the second-highest career field-goal percentage (.596) in Orange basketball history. I was a second-team Academic All-American in my senior year. I started for the Portland Trail Blazers during my rookie season in the NBA. Who am I?

Go on. We've got time.

What? You give up?

The answer is…Bill Smith. Yeah, Bill Smith.

"Who's Bill Smith?" repeated Bill Smith. "I know what you mean. It sounds like a phony name. My wife's name is Mary. So, when we sign in at hotels and motels, as 'Bill and Mary Smith,' the front desk people look at us and say, 'And you don't have any luggage, right?' But what am I going to do? That's my name. I'm Bill Smith."

And not so long ago, Bill Smith—who stood all of six-foot-11 and weighed every ounce of 225 pounds—was a pretty good player for the Syracuse Orangemen. And never mind that he's been all but forgotten.

"I have been kind of lost," he said, "in the mists of time."

It turns out that Smith suited up for Roy Danforth's first three SU clubs between 1968-69 and 1970-71, during which time the Orange went 40-35. And, oh, he did have his moments.

For instance, there was the night of January 14, 1971, when he scored those 47 points—to break Dave Bing's record of 46—against poor Lafayette and its overmatched six-foot-six center, Ron Moyer, before 2,015 Manley Field House witnesses. Or rather, take what happened in the hours after the last of his 17 field goals and 13 free throws fell through the net.

"The guys took me out for a little drinking celebration and I ended up in a chugging contest with Bernie Fine," said Smith. And, no, Fine was not a Syracuse assistant coach at the time; rather he was merely a civilian. "I thought I was a big drinker, but what I didn't know was that Bernie was just throwing his beers over his shoulder while I was downing mine. The last thing I remember was stumbling out of the pub with my jacket on backwards.

"It wasn't pretty. You know how, when you've had too much to drink, the ceiling starts spinning on you? Well, that was me. I ended up hugging the porcelain convenience. I got so sick that I vowed I'd never drink again. And guess what? I haven't had another drink of alcohol since that night. Since January. 14, 1971. I swear to God."

You might imagine that was the most memorable night of Bill Smith's basketball career. Either that, or the night in 1968 when he scored 41 invisible points (in his second-ever varsity game) for the Orangemen in the very contest in which Calvin Murphy scored 68 for Niagara. Either that, or the night in 1971 when he scored 17 points (a month or so into his pro career) for Portland in the first quarter against Milwaukee's Kareem Abdul-Jabbar...and then added just one more before fouling out in the second quarter.

But you would be wrong. Because the real never-to-be-forgotten night of Bill Smith's basketball career took place on February 14, 1970, which was, in a strange twist of landmark fate, the occasion of his 21st birthday.

"We were playing at West Virginia," Bill recalled, "and I got into a little scuffle."

Smith punched one of the game's officials, Herb Young. That's what he did. With 61 seconds left in the game, with Smith having been called for a questionable fifth foul, and with Smith insisting that he'd just been slapped in the face by Young, who'd been offended by the complaining Orangeman's salty tongue, Smith hauled off and punched the referee. And the joint went up for grabs.

"Immediately, there are these two cops, one on each of my arms," Smith remembered. "But I shake them off and when I do, a fan grabs me by my feet and tackles me to the ground. And just like that, there must have been 500 people on the court with fistfights like you couldn't believe.

"My mother, father, sister and fiancee were there. My dad got the guy who'd tackled me and was punching him in the face. My sister was out there, swinging her purse. Somebody had ripped off my sneaker and was hitting me in the head with it. Greg 'Kid' Kohls, who everybody always thought was so mild-mannered, uppercutted one guy once and then he uppercutted him again before the guy decided he'd had enough. It was wild. It was a melee. You really had to see it to believe it."

As could be expected, the game was declared over at that point, the Mountaineers were awarded a 94-84 victory . . . and the Orangemen were holed up in their locker room for a good hour and a half before it was deemed safe enough for them to be given a police escort off campus.

"I'll never forget Danforth," Smith recalled. "He said, 'Smitty, you hit the ref!' And I said, 'Yeah, but he slapped me.' And he said, 'Smitty, you hit the ref!' And I said, 'Yeah, but he slapped me.' We just kept going back and forth like that."

It turned out that Smith—who was advised by Danforth the next afternoon to quit school and join the Army—was kicked off the team for the rest of the season, suffering in effect just a soft five-game suspension for his stunning punch. But he returned the following year, his senior campaign, led the Orangemen in both scoring (22.7) and rebounding (14.5), and was chosen by Portland with the 42nd pick in the 1971 NBA Draft. Smith later moved on to Oregon where he still lives (and works for Smith Barney) with his family in Medford.

And all this time later, he wonders.

"You know, every year the people at Syracuse send a copy of the press guide to me," Smith said. "And every year when I look through it and check out the records, I see that, all things considered, I'm still one of the school's better players. But I think I've been kind of overlooked. I'm not bitter about it, but it's true. I don't know. Maybe it's because of that fight at West Virginia."

A little theme music, please…

I'm the only Orangeman ever to have punched a referee during a game and become not infamous, but nearly anonymous. Who am I?

The answer is…Bill Smith. And you can look it up.

ROY'S RUNTS

You can't teach height, so Roy Danforth didn't bother for a while there in the early '70s when so few of his Orangemen needed to duck while walking through a doorway.

"Why were we called 'Roy's Runts'?" repeated Mike Lee. "Because I was one forward and Mark Wadach was the other forward. That's why."

It was amazing, but true. During the 1970-71 and 1971-72 seasons, Lee (at six-foot-three) and Wadach (at six-foot-two) started underneath...and flourished. More remarkable yet, Bob Dooms, at six-foot-five, was the starting center in the second of those two campaigns.

Oh, and when the Orangemen went "big" in the senior year of Lee and Wadach, they went all of six-foot-seven (Rudy Hackett), six-foot-five (Dooms) and six-foot-three (Lee) across the front with Wadach moving into the backcourt with the six-foot-three Dennis DuVal. So, even then—with a starting lineup that suddenly averaged six-foot-four per man—"big" SU was still...small.

"You know, our lack of size would work to our benefit," declared Lee, who averaged 16.3 points throughout his three-year varsity career during which he started every game. "Other teams would see me and Mark walk on the floor and they'd be, like, 'How good can they be?' I used to hear the guys Mark was guarding say, 'Give me the ball. I've got a little man on me.' And then they'd throw it into him and Mark would either strip it away or block the shot. He was an unbelievable jumper."

Oh, they were a feisty bunch, those Runts were. In fact, during the Lee-Wadach era, SU went 65-18 and to two NITs and one NCAA Tournament. And by March of 1973, they were ranked as high as No. 13 in all the land.

"We'd get beaten up sometimes, sure," said Lee, who came to Syracuse to play both baseball and basketball from Windsor High School just outside of Binghamton, N.Y. "But the other teams would get tired, too. We used to run and press the whole game. The biggest thing with Roy's Runts was we'd get up and down the court all night long.

"And we played together so well. We were all pretty good athletes who could handle the ball and shoot and rebound and run and play defense. People tend to get too specialized today. But not us. We were hard to defend because we could do a little bit of everything."

Everything, that is, but grow. And when they bumped into Maryland's six-foot-11 Tom McMillen and six-foot-10 Len Elmore three times in a span of 30 games—each of which they lost by the progressively worse scores of 71-65, 91-76 and 91-75—the Runts' vertically challenged condition hurt them badly.

Worse, however, was their road run-in with Massachusetts's Julius Erving on February 22, 1971, at old Curry Hicks Cage. While it's true that Doctor J was "only" six-foot-seven, on that night against those Orangemen he seemed a foot taller.

"I remember Coach Danforth's scouting report," Lee said. "He told us, 'They've got this guy named Erving, who's a pretty good player.' That was it. That was the report. Well, he was pretty good, all right, because he went for 36 points and 32 rebounds, and you can look that up. I mean, he was just jumping right over us. Everybody guarded him, but nobody guarded him, if you know what I mean."

UMass won that game, 86-71. But if you remove those old Redmen and the McMillen-Elmore Terrapins, only 11 schools—American, Fordham, Holy Cross (twice), Louisville, Michigan, Penn State (twice), Pennsylvania, Pittsburgh, St. Francis, Temple (twice) and Tennessee—managed to knock off Roy's Runts in the three years that Lee and Wadach and all the rest looked up, literally, to their competition.

"Sometimes," Lee said, "I think the other teams took us lightly. You know, because we were small."

That was a mistake. Yep, a big mistake.

DANFORTH GOT HIS MAN

It's been said that recruiting is like shaving. You'd better do it every day, or you'll look like a bum.

That submitted, you should know that Roy Danforth, who preceded Jim Boeheim as the Orangemen's head coach, was no bum. Oddly attired, maybe. But no bum.

"I lived in Newcastle, which is a part of Westbury in Nassau County," Dennis DuVal said. "It wasn't an affluent part of town, let's put it that way. Anyway, the first time I met Roy Danforth was the day he drove up to my house.

"I remember he was standing there at the door, wearing some real bright plaid pants. And he had two parts in his hair. My mother took a look at him and told me, 'You better go out there and get that man real quick before something happens to him.' He was dressed a little bit different than the people in my neighborhood, if you get what I'm saying."

OK, so maybe the guy's wardrobe looked like something out of "Laugh-In." But Danforth, SU's coach from 1968-69 through 1975-76, wanted DuVal, who was fast becoming a legend at Westbury High School. And his notoriously goofy threads were not going to stop him from hitting the recruiting trail in pursuit of the fabulous Double-D.

Nor, it so happens, would a little water.

"When I was a senior in high school, I played in an all-star tournament in Schenectady called the Schoolboy Classic," said DuVal, who'd been recruited by Syracuse since his sophomore year. "There were four states represented among the players—Massachusetts, Connecticut, Rhode Island and New York. And I was named the MVP."

"As I recall, there were about 200 coaches there and Danforth was one of them. So, this one particular game is over and I'm in the shower. I mean, I'm physically in the shower, naked, standing under the water. And I turn around...and there's Danforth. In the shower with me, fully dressed. I don't know what he was wearing that day, but I do know his shoes were getting wet. I do remember that."

It so happened that DuVal, a six-foot-three guard with enough talent to eventually become a second-round NBA draft choice of the then-Washington Bullets, was scheduled to visit the Syracuse campus in a couple of weeks. And Danforth, knowing that every other coach on the grounds had seen DuVal light up the competition, was merely protecting the turf he'd been panting over for three years.

"So, there I am in the shower," DuVal recalled. "And there's Danforth in there with me. And I say, 'Give me a minute, Coach. I'll be right out.' I mean, what else could I do? Like I said, there were 200 coaches there, but he was the only one in the shower. I hadn't mailed my letter of intent, but I'd already made up my mind that I was going to Syracuse. But Roy didn't know that and, I guess, he was just making sure that nobody else got to me."

Danforth's tenacity was well directed because DuVal ended up leading the Orangemen in scoring in both his junior (19.5) and senior (22.2) campaigns. And he still holds SU's homecourt record for most field goals attempted and made in a single game after having gone 18-for-30 in the Orangemen's 110-53 victory over Bucknell on January 23, 1974.

Perhaps, then, the old Syracuse ramrod—who understood that coaches have to shave and recruit every day—can be forgiven for once upon a time standing in Dennis DuVal's shower.

"Roy was different," DuVal said. "A nice guy, but different."

Bright plaid pants. Two parts in his hair. Wet shoes. Yeah, he was different, all right. But who would recognize Roy Danforth any other way?

SWEET D, THE SHOWMAN

Believe it or not, there once was a time when college basketball coaches were a fairly loose bunch.

Abe Lemons, who ran things at a few different schools, once opened his weekly television show by dramatically climbing out of a casket and proclaiming, "We ain't dead yet." Frank Layden, the top dog at Niagara, allowed Calvin Murphy to twirl batons as part of the Purple Eagles' pregame entertainment. Press Maravich thought it was a dandy idea for his son, Pete, to make like the Harlem Globetrotters' magical Meadowlark Lemon prior to LSU contests.

And then there was Roy Danforth, the Orangemen's impresario of a head man, who looked at Dennis DuVal and saw his very own "Pistol."

"It was a layup-line warmup drill," recalled DuVal of what would become his signature. "Before the games, I'd stand in the middle of the foul line and guys would cut off me and I'd give them passes. It was just spur-of-the-moment stuff. Whatever pass I felt like throwing, I threw. Between my legs. Around my back. Whatever. We were actually pretty good, and the crowd loved it."

It was good old-fashioned showbiz played out to the theme from *Shaft* and other tunes of the times. That's what it was. Fun. And while DuVal, a six-foot-three guard who played for SU from 1971-72 through 1973-74, was the star of the production, Danforth was its originator.

"We were screwing around in practice one day before the coaches got there," said DuVal, who evolved into an All-American for the Orangemen by the time he was a senior. "And Danforth caught us. I guess he liked what he saw because he told us to do it as part of our pregame warmups.

Hey, he was the coach, so we did it. It got the fans pumped up. And it got us pumped up, too."

The Sweet D Show, unveiled only before home contests, ran for all three of DuVal's varsity seasons. But, truth be told, it wasn't restricted only to the hoo-ha preceding the opening tip because Dennis—who would eventually become the Chief of Police in Syracuse—was known to get fairly creative after the ball went up for good.

"Yeah, you could say I was a fancy passer," he said. "During the games, I'd throw passes behind my back and through my legs. Sure, I did that."

And Danforth, sitting over there on the bench, had no problems with that?

"Well," DuVal said, "on some occasions, he did."

Not often enough, though, to stop The Show.

It Was All Happening at the Zoo

For a while there, death and taxes had almost nothing on Manley Field House, which evolved into nearly as sure a thing for visitors as a bellyache after some bad egg salad. Why, during the last 10 full seasons that the Orangemen played in the old barn, Syracuse went 123-6. And four of those six losses were by a total of seven points.

SU, then, was as tough to beat at home as the English. Nevertheless, in 1980, the Orangemen—with Jim Boeheim grousing all the way—moved into the spanking-new Carrier Dome, where they went 25-6 in their first 31 games...meaning they'd have to go 98-0 in their next 98 contests to match what they'd done on their way out of Manley. And they didn't.

"When you get 30,000 people in the Dome, that's a big crowd," admitted Jimmy Lee. "But I've heard people who've come in with visiting teams say it's not that big of a homecourt advantage, because the fans are not as close as they were at Manley."

And how close were those fans in that dingy joint?

"Close enough," Lee said, "to put their elbows on the court."

He'd know, of course. Jimmy Lee, after all, played his entire Syracuse career—1972-73 through 1974-75—at Manley Field House, where his deadly jumpers pierced the dusty air with enough accuracy to help him score 1,165 points during his time in an SU uniform.

"Those were great days," remembered Lee, whose three varsity clubs combined to go 33-3 at home. "First of all, because Manley was built for the football team to practice in, the floor was laid on a dirt field, so there was always dust in the air. I'd run into guys from other teams years later who'd say, 'I didn't have any problems in that place in the first half. But in the second half, man, I couldn't breathe.' I'd just laugh.

"And, second of all, we had 'The Zoo,' which was a pack of loud and rowdy fans right next to the visitors' bench. When opposing teams would call a timeout, the players couldn't even hear the coach because 'The Zoo' would be going nuts. I mean, the fans were right on top of the court. They were in touching distance, they were so close."

They were close enough, too, to witness some bizarre episodes. Like, for instance, the one involving Jimmy's older brother, Mike, a senior, during SU's raucous 80-70 upset of ninth-ranked St. John's on Valentine's Day in 1973.

"We come out like a house on fire (leading, 29-8), but in the second half they're slowly catching us," said Jimmy. "So, Mike is coming down the floor and he's called for a foul (with SU ahead by only 65-62). And he's so mad, he kicks the ball over the backboard and almost into the last row of the upper deck. Well, Frank Mulzoff, the St. John's coach, sees this and he goes crazy, absolutely crazy, trying to get the referee's attention.

"Right then, Roy Danforth throws a towel onto the floor and as soon as he does, he turns to one of the ball boys and starts hollering at him. 'Why'd you throw that towel on the floor? What are you doing? What's wrong with you?' I mean, Coach D throws it and he's blaming it on the poor kid, who doesn't know what's going on. And the ref is standing there, watching the whole thing."

The other of the game's two officials? Because he was reporting the foul to the scorer's table, he had his back to the court, too. Meanwhile, with the roaring Mulzoff's face turning blue, the fans—and there were 8,944 of them in the pews—shuffled the ball back down to the floor, bucket-brigade style...and by the time the refs turned around, it was on the floor as if nothing had happened.

"Oh, it was great," said Jimmy, then a sophomore guard but now the vice-president of a Syracuse-area petroleum supplier. "It was unbelievable. There was no technical foul and we ended up winning. I still don't know why Mike did that. I mean, he didn't do stuff like that. But I've got to tell you, it was a perfect kick."

A perfect kick, that is, during another perfect Manley Field House season. The Orangemen went 11-0 at home that year. And they'd gone 13-0 during the previous campaign. And they'd go almost perfect, 10-1, in the next. And folks used to think that beating Joe Louis in Detroit was tough.

MAYBE THEY COULD
HAVE TUNNELED OUT

Jim Valvano, who died of cancer in 1993 at the age of 47, was famous for the 1983 NCAA Tournament championship he won while coaching at North Carolina State. But the man had a wit, too. And few will forget that.

It turned out that Valvano needed his sense of humor back on January 23, 1974, because that was the day he took his Bucknell Bisons—5-7 at the time—into Manley Field House to serve as speed bags for the Orangemen of Dennis DuVal, Rudy Hackett and Jimmy Lee.

He was just a kid then—a 27-year-old in his second season as the lead dog at Bucknell, a gig that would propel him first to Iona and then onto N.C. State. And, boy, did Jimmy V get schooled in the dusty structure where SU had won 40 of its previous 42 games.

"At halftime, we were only down by eight," Valvano recalled years later. "Eight touchdowns."

The final score? It was Syracuse 110, Bucknell 53. And during the rout, DuVal took 30 shots from the field and buried 18 of them. No Orangeman, before or since, has ever attempted or converted that many field goals in any game ever played in Syracuse.

"Manley Field House," Valvano said, "was the only building I knew where they locked the doors from the inside until after the game. That way, the bus drivers outside couldn't help the visiting team escape."

He may have been onto something. Throughout the 18 full seasons in which the Orangemen played at old Manley— a round structure that had been built as a practice facility for the Syracuse football team—their record was 190-29, and during that time they posted winning streaks of 57 and 36 games.

But none of that history meant much way back when to Valvano, who was more than a little peeved as the Syracuse guys ran past, dunked over and more or less laughed at his poor Bisons.

"Syracuse was a gracious host," he'd later write in his autobiography, *Valvano*. "They ended up beating us, 110-53, and the Orange coach, Roy Danforth, led the student body in cheers when they got a 55-point lead. Walks right by me, leads them in cheers, walks back. Is this a fun profession or what? Then afterward he came in with a stat sheet to show me that everybody on their team played. I thought: Is this depression necessary?"

Suffice it to say, Valvano didn't bring his Bucknell outfit back to Syracuse the following season. And after that, he was gone—to Iona, later to N.C. State, and finally to the publishing house with his autobiography. All those years later, Jimmy V's miserable Manley memories had not faded.

1975 FINAL FOUR:
THE ORANGEMEN WORE
THE BLUE COLLARS

They were basketball players back there in 1975, sure. Rudy Hackett, Jimmy Lee, Chris Sease—all of them. But they were their school's Final Four pioneers, too.

Indeed, before Carmelo Anthony and his cheery side-kicks won in New Orleans in 2003...before the 'Cuse Was In The House at the Meadowlands in 1996...before SU had its heart broken by Keith Smart at the Louisiana Superdome in 1987...before all of that, there were those other Orangemen.

And, oh, what a ride they gave central and upstate New York. All the way, that is, to San Diego, where they stepped into a starry field with regal UCLA, aristocratic Kentucky and highbrow Louisville.

"It was the blue bloods against the blue collars," said Earnie Seibert, Syracuse's center at the time, nearly 30 years later.

It turns out that the Orangemen lost to both the immense Wildcats (95-79 in the semifinals) and the rangy Cardinals (96-88 in overtime in the consolation affair) during that Final Four. But in the big picture, the scores matter less than the fact that Syracuse traveled so deep into March.

The Orangemen, after all, had played just one Top 20 club, Providence, throughout the regular season—and had lost to it by 23 points. They had dropped back-to-back games in Manley Field House to Rutgers and West Virginia and performed before a crowd of some 2,000 in their next home contest. They had entered the ECAC postseason playoffs with an unremarkable 18-7 record and had been beaten by those Scarlet Knights and Mountaineers—and by Canisius, too—in a span of 10 February days.

"There was a time when it was looking like a lackluster year," said Steve Shaw, now a Syracuse-area lawyer but then a six-foot-four senior forward. "It was kind of like, 'What's going on here?' People were beginning to write us off. But then, I don't know, we just rode the wave."

And that wave—which transported the Orangemen past LaSalle (in overtime), Kansas State and North Carolina (again, in overtime) in NCAA Tournament play—carried them to Southern California. And upon arrival? Well, it was then, after they'd unveiled their bad haircuts, odd physiques, and curious wardrobes, that they were deemed to be the beggars at the feast.

"We were a bunch of guys who didn't look like we were from a top, elite program," said Shaw. "For instance, when we played North Carolina in Providence, they arrived all decked out in their baby blue and their checkered blazers. Well, we dressed like individuals, you know what I mean? Like, Bug Williams had his shades. Stuff like that. So, when we got to San Diego, some of the writers took shots at us."

"We were the underdogs, and I guess you have to write something," said Kevin King, who was a six-foot-four junior swingman. "We had some characters on that team, yeah. But mostly we were just a bunch of kids, who weren't really media savvy, playing ball and having fun. Were we a motley crew? Probably. But we were no more motley than half the teams in college basketball."

"People saw us out there," said Seibert, "and it was like we'd crashed the party or something."

If so, it was the party to crash, even if the 1975 Final Four didn't have the sis-boom-bah properties of the 2003

Final Four. For example, while back-to-back crowds of 54,000-plus folks were in the Superdome to watch Anthony's eventual champions knock off Texas and then Kansas, the two gatherings at the San Diego Sports Arena numbered 12,983 and 15,151. And the capacity in that joint was 15,200.

"Back then, the Final Four wasn't hyped like it is now," said King, who is the head basketball coach at Westhill High School in suburban Syracuse. "We had newspaper and radio and TV coverage like we'd never seen before, but it was probably only about one-tenth of what it is at today's Final Fours.

"Don't get me wrong. The Final Four was a big deal and we were excited to go, but what was really great was going to San Diego. I don't know if it would have meant as much to us if the Final Four was in Philadelphia, like it was the next year. I mean, Philly's a nice town, but we were going all the way across the country to California. That was a big part of the allure, no question."

Once there, the Orangemen got pounded on the boards, 57-40, by Kentucky's massive squad and were then edged in OT by Louisville, which survived Lee's would-be winning jumper from the foul line that fell off the rim at the end of regulation.

So, lugging an 0-2 record in the program's first-ever Final Four appearance, they came home. Eventually. You see, Mexico dozed just a few miles to the south, Las Vegas was sitting close by in the desert, Los Angeles was only a couple of hours to the north, and Black's Beach (where bathing suits were, as they say, optional, and the naked girls were many) was right down the street. As such, some of the Orangemen, wide-eyed and lugging few school books, were in no hurry to return to Syracuse.

It happened that Seibert, the six-foot-nine, 260-pound sophomore center, had no choice in the matter. First of all, he'd sprained his back after a scary fall during the Louisville affair that resulted in his being lugged off the floor on a stretcher and then being driven to a local hospital. And, secondly, his wife—make that, his very pregnant wife, Laurie—was waiting back home. So, he headed East.

But Shaw and King and certain others? Well, with Coach Roy Danforth's blessing—and remembering that NCAA mores were different in 1975—they cashed in their return airline tickets and used the money to fund a bit of sightseeing before sooner or later wending their way back to central New York. Shaw and Billy DeMarle, for instance, pushed on to LA and then to San Francisco; for his part, King hitch-hiked his way from San Diego to Steamboat Springs, Colorado, to Omaha, Nebraska, to Syracuse.

"When did I get back to campus?" repeated King, forever a free spirit, but then an even freer one who favored leather jackets and a haircut that was straight from the Prince Valiant page in his barber's manual. "Three weeks? A month? Two weeks? Somewhere in there. I don't remember. I guess I'd have to check my records. My thumb and I got back after a while, but I missed the team banquet."

Thus, did he lose out on the salutes and the toasts and the slaps on the back. And there were a fair number of those, because the 1975 Orangemen were their school's pioneers—their school's Final Four pioneers—and they deserved all of the huzzahs they received.

Those who chose to listen in 1987, 1996 and 2003 could still hear the echoes.

OLD SHOOTERS NEVER DIE

The coaches will talk forever about defense and rebounding, about passing and all the rest. But basketball, first and foremost, is about putting the ball in the hoop. And to do that, you need shooters. And the Orangemen have had their fair share.

Tuppy Hayman, Mel Besdin, Dave Bing, Jim Boeheim, George Hicker, Greg Kohls, Steve Shaw, Jimmy Lee, Hal Cohen, Marty Headd, Gene Waldron, Greg Monroe, Marius Januaryulis, Preston Shumpert, Gerry McNamara, and so on. Anybody foolish enough to have engaged any of those guys—and certain others, too—in a game of H-O-R-S-E would surely have left the court with a lighter wallet.

You don't, after all, tug on Superman's cape...you don't spit into the wind...and you don't call out a shooter. Nope. Never.

"I loved to shoot," said Lee, the six-foot-one guard whose marksmanship helped the Orangemen advance to the 1975 Final Four. "I'd shoot all the time. I'd shoot for hours. I'd shoot and shoot and shoot. I used to shoot foul shots in my back yard at home all the time. I once made 423 in a row with my sister rebounding for me. It took about an hour and a half. I still can't believe she stayed out there the whole time."

It all paid off, because not only did Lee—who followed his older brother, Mike, to SU from Kirkwood, N.Y.—score 1,165 points in his three-year varsity career with the Orangemen, but the countless jumpers helped grow his confidence.

"The best shooter at Syracuse?" said Lee, whose 35 points led all scorers in the San Diego Final Four. "Me. You will not get me to say that anybody at that school has ever been a better shooter. But that's a shooter's mind for you."

Hicker, perhaps SU's greatest shooter from the '60s, can identify with Lee, because not only did he light up opposing defenses while scoring 1,245 points during his three-year varsity career, he sent shivers down the backs of a whole bunch of future generations.

"Boeheim can verify this," said Hicker of the long-time Syracuse coach who was a senior when George was a sophomore. "I'd go back for the Alumni Game every year, and the day before the game I'd shoot with whichever player wanted to shoot. And I'm talking about the active players. Greg Monroe. Mike Hopkins. David Johnson. Allen Griffin. All of them.

"And I got beat once. And that was by Derrick Coleman, believe it or not. It was Coleman and Stevie Thompson and David Johnson and me. We were in Manley Field House and it came down to Coleman and me. And I said, 'Do you want to go first?' And typical of Coleman, he said, 'I don't care.' I mean, he's never cared about much, has he?

"So, I went first and hit a non-inspired six-for-nine from three-point range. He started off four-for-six, so he had to make his last three to win. And he did it. He made all three...and I'll never forget what he did next. As soon as that last shot fell, Derrick ran off the floor, he ran through Manley and he ran out the side of the gym never to be seen again. He wasn't about to give me a rematch."

That was back in 1989 and Hicker, now a Southern California businessman, was already on the far side of 40. Not that it mattered. He was a shooter, remember. One of the finest Syracuse shooters of all time. And great shooters don't die easy. They just keep taking aim...and firing.

SU's Soup and Sandwich

They were Syracuse's Hope and Crosby, its soup and sandwich, its Pete and Repeat. There was Stockton and Malone, there was Sam and Dave, there was Watson and Holmes. And there was Bouie and Louie.

Or was it Louie and Bouie? All these years later—they haven't suited up for the Orangemen since 1980—each insists that the other deserves top billing. As if it matters.

"I couldn't ask for a better teammate," Louis Orr said of Roosevelt Bouie. "I couldn't ask for a better friend."

"If Louis was a mean and terrible and nasty person, it might be a bad thing to be linked with him forever," Roosevelt Bouie said of Louis Orr. "If you told me I was linked with Ned, the wino, I'd be upset. But Louis? Louis is my friend."

They played side by side for four seasons, scoring 3,047 points and grabbing 1,868 rebounds between them. Or an average of 25.8 points and 15.8 rebounds per game, every game, while crafting a won-lost record of 100-18—including an astonishing 55-1 in Manley Field House—and earning four NCAA Tournament berths. As such, if they weren't the finest pair of Orangemen, long term, in the history of the Syracuse basketball program, well, then perhaps a bear's bathroom fixtures aren't covered in bark, after all.

"He was a presence from Day One," said Orr, the six-foot-nine forward from Cincinnati, of Bouie. "Defensively. Offensively. Physically. Rebounding. I mean to tell you, Roosevelt was the guy you had to deal with when you played Syracuse. I was real thin, so with him just being on the court, he took the pounding off me and freed me up to do some things."

One of those things was to demonstrate his savvy, the kind of which (coupled with his talent) would eventually allow Orr to play a combined eight NBA campaigns for the Pacers and Knicks. But that he did only after thoroughly impressing Bouie in Syracuse.

"I remember this one game during our senior year when Louis ended up with no points, about 14 rebounds and about 11 assists," said Bouie, the six-foot-11 center from Kendall, N.Y. "And all of those assists were to me because I had the weakest link guarding me and Louis thought I should get the ball. Well, I did get the ball. All night, thanks to him, and we won. That's all that mattered to him.

"That spoke volumes to me. I mean, I already knew Louis. But everything he did in that game reaffirmed what I'd believed about him. He just told me, 'Hey, there'll be a game when the guy I'm guarding won't be able to hold me and I'll get my points then.' Everything about Louis was the team. Everything."

They were buddies, the two of them. Bouie and Louie, so quiet, dressed at adjoining lockers in Manley Field House. Louie and Bouie, so polite, lived next door to each other at Skytop. Bouie and Louie...Louie and Bouie. Where you saw one, you likely saw the other.

"In those days, we didn't have a lot in terms of resources," said Orr. "So when one had, both had. We shared everything. Cake, food, cars. When he got a care package from home, it was as good as mine. When I got a care package from home, it was as good as his. That's just the way it was."

Eventually, the duo did split up as Orr took his skills to the NBA while Bouie left for Europe, where he dunked on a lot of foreign heads for 13-plus campaigns. But in 1988, when each was 30 years of age, they teamed again, suiting up for Riunite in the Italian city of Reggio Emilia, 75 minutes south of Milan. And for the better part of a season, they presented a revival of the Bouie and Louie Show. Or, the Louie and Bouie Show. Whatever.

"That was probably the most enjoyable time we ever spent together," said Bouie. "We'd go out to dinner after practice at this restaurant that belonged to one of our teammates, Luciano Giumbini. We'd sit down around seven o'clock and we'd finish around midnight. We'd eat and then we'd talk about everything you could imagine."

They're still talking, of course. A couple of times a month, anyway—Bouie an internationally backgrounded businessman; Orr a head basketball coach, first at Siena and then at Seton Hall. And the conversations always seem to naturally pick up, one from the other.

"We are, basically, mild-mannered guys," said Orr, "and our regard for each other has grown from the very first day we met as freshmen."

"We were pretty much raised the same way," said Bouie. "We've always been respectful of people, and that includes each other to this very day."

Bouie and Louie. Louie and Bouie. Friends, whatever the order. Wonderful basketball players, too.

PASS THE MAYO

If Leo Eisner, along with so many other members of the Syracuse University Hardwood Club, were into cold cuts these days as much as they were once upon a time, they might be hauled away in handcuffs by the NCAA's far-too-serious gendarmes.

Indeed, assuming that Eisner and his gang were still up to their old tricks, they would be considered scalawags here in the 21st century. But between the late '60s and early '80s, they were just a bunch of nice folks with mayonnaise to spare.

You've heard of a chicken in every pot? Eisner and the Hardwood Club believed in a sandwich in every hand. That is, in every basketball player's hand.

"Back then," Eisner said, "it was all perfectly legal."

"It" was feeding the Orangemen—and, later, certain among the Orangemen's foes, too—following games at Manley Field House and for a while at the Carrier Dome. Nothing fancy, mind you. Just sandwiches and chips and soda and pretzels. But that would probably be enough to warrant NCAA investigation in the here and now.

"We fed the team after every home game for at least 10 years," said Eisner, who capped his 32nd campaign as a Hardwood Club member by watching SU win the 2003 NCAA Tournament. "Wait, more than 10 years. One season we decided to start inviting the visiting teams. We asked Georgetown, and John Thompson always politely turned us down. And Rollie Massimino always said no at Villanova. But Seton Hall loved it. You know, it was a low-budget program, so this allowed them to save money. Bill Raftery was coaching them back then, and he always brought his team in for a bite."

"Providence did it. Connecticut did it. And a bunch of others. It only cost about $75 a game for the whole spread, but the best part was that the players from both sides mingled together and got to know each other. As far as we could tell, Syracuse was the only school in the country that ever did that. It was great."

Well, yeah. The postgame smorgasbord—which ended when Carrier Dome operatives insisted that they provide the food...and at a higher cost, yet—did foster camaraderie and friendship and goodwill. But it also produced some bickering (good-natured, for sure) between Roosevelt Bouie and Louis Orr, the two pals who played together as Orangemen from 1976-77 through 1979-80.

"My wife, Billie, would bake cakes for every one of those home games," Leo recalled. "I mean, every one for more than 10 years. Well, Roosevelt would sidle up to her and say, 'Mrs. E, would you make a chocolate cake the next time?' And Louis would say, 'No, Mrs. E. I don't like chocolate. Make it lemon.' So every game, Billie would have to alternate cakes. Chocolate, lemon...lemon, chocolate...."

Billie's baking must have been something. The Louie and Bouie Show, after all, went 100-18 during its four-year run. Serious cake power, that.

HE COULDA BEEN A CONTENDER...
ER, MAVERICK

Somebody has to be the greatest Orangeman never to have played in the NBA, and with apologies to Jim Boeheim, his own self, Roosevelt Bouie, the six-foot-11 center out of Kendall, N.Y., just may be that guy. To be fair, though, an asterisk must come with his title because it was Bouie's choice, rather than the other side's, not to suit up with the big boys.

"There was a time when I thought I'd like to play in the NBA," Bouie admitted. "But I'm a people person. I like to be treated like a person, and in the NBA sometimes the players are treated by the team as if they're not the No. 1 concern. Italy is a smaller country. It's a smaller league. The people are like your next-door neighbor.

"I got spoiled at Syracuse. After being there and playing there, Italy was the closest thing to a situation that I felt I could live with. I only went there for a year or two. But after about the fifth year of telling myself I was going to go back to the States, I said to myself, 'Roosevelt, who are you kidding?' I felt right at home, so I stayed."

He stayed, all right. For 13-plus seasons, he stayed—12 in Italy (where he became a much revered, and generously compensated, superstar), one in Spain and part of another in Switzerland. And in all that time, Bouie claims to rarely have given the Dallas Mavericks, who'd chosen him with the 34th pick in the 1980 NBA draft, much thought.

"There's an old saying that if you walk around looking backwards, you're either going to step on something or fall into something," said Bouie, who would become the first high-profile American to spend his entire professional career in Europe. "And I've never been particularly interested in doing either of those. So, I always kept my eye on where I was going, not where I used to be."

As such, it has hardly bothered him that—including the latest, Carmelo Anthony—a total of 29 former Orangemen have competed in the NBA, and that he is not among that number. Lou Spicer, who scored one and only one NBA point (for the Providence Steamrollers in 1946)...yes. Roosevelt Bouie, who played against the likes of Arvydas Sabonis, Bob McAdoo, Darryl Dawkins, Toni Kukoc and Danny Ferry in Europe...no.

Still, the numbers suggest that Bouie is clearly SU's finest non-NBA player, because at the conclusion of the 2002-03 season, he was No. 2 on the school's all-time list of shots blocked (327), No. 6 in rebounds grabbed (987) and tied for No. 13 in points scored (1,560). And, remember, SU has been playing this game since 1901.

In fact, of the 25 members of Syracuse's All-Century Team, only Bouie, Vinnie Cohen, Vic Hanson, Greg Kohls, Jimmy Lee and Joe Schwartzer failed to dress in the NBA. And Hanson and Schwartzer—who played for the Orangemen in the teens and the '20s, respectively—had a pretty good reason: The league didn't come along until 1946.

But again, make no mistake here. In Bouie's case, the plug was pulled by the athlete, not by the NBA.

"Roosevelt could have played 10, 12, 14 years in the league if he'd wanted to," said Louis Orr, the former Orangeman who suited up for eight seasons for the Indiana Pacers and New York Knicks and would, therefore, seem to know of what he speaks. "He had good size, he was a defensive presence who could block shots and change games, he could rebound and he could get up and down the floor.

"Guys like that are commodities. And he looked after his body, too. Roosevelt was a professional. He was a character guy, someone you didn't have to worry about doing the wrong thing. He would have come to work and done his job every day. But Europe was his niche, and if you know Roosevelt, you know he's going to do what's comfortable for him."

So, Bouie headed across the pond and upon arrival, he immersed himself in his new world. Indeed, the big man speaks fluent Italian, knows Spanish nearly as well and can read any French newspaper over any morning croissant. Moreover, many of his business dealings have European roots. And another thing: As Bouie played a schedule of only some 35 games per year over there, his knees—which are on the far side of 40—neither creak nor wobble when it rains.

Nevertheless, even after rebuffing American basketball and its celebrity entrapments, there were times when Roosevelt, the nouveau Italian who did a fair amount of fly-fishing in the Adriatic Mountains, would still wonder if he wasn't walking along Marshall Street.

"In Syracuse, it was very difficult for Louis and me to go to places and not get recognized," Bouie recalled. "But I get over to Italy and I say, 'Finally, I'm so far away from everybody, no one will single me out.' Well, right away I pull into a gas station in Bologna and the guy says to me, 'Bouie!' I say, 'Yeah, how'd you know?' So, he showed me some newspapers and there I was. And then something else hit me, too: I'm tall, I'm black and I'm in Italy. I guess I stood out a little bit over there."

Just as he might have stood out once upon a time in, oh, Dallas.

DOLPH COULD HAVE USED A SEAT BELT

He'd waited, and not patiently, for three years to see his son get some serious minutes with the Syracuse University basketball team. And by his own admission, Dolph Schayes got crankier and crankier as the time slowly...creaked...by.

"To be honest with you," Dolph said, "I wasn't happy. I'd be sitting in the stands and I'd be muttering, 'What's the matter with Boeheim? How come he doesn't use Danny more? He could use him, high/low, with Bouie.' That kind of stuff. Instead of just making Danny a foil for Bouie in practice, Boeheim should have played him more. At least, that's what I always thought."

As it turned out, Roosevelt Bouie, SU's wonderful center, graduated in 1980. And Shaker High School's heavily recruited Sam Perkins decided to leave Latham, N.Y., that year for North Carolina and Dean Smith's Tar Heels rather than for Syracuse and Jim Boeheim's Orangemen.

And just like that, Dolph got his wish, because his son, Danny—a brainy six-foot-11 senior, and the happy beneficiary of a fabulous basketball gene pool—became SU's undisputed man in the middle for the 1980-81 campaign. And he took full advantage, averaging 14.6 points and 8.4 rebounds, and ultimately becoming a first-round draft choice of the Utah Jazz.

"That was quite a season for me," recalled Dolph, certainly one of the NBA's greatest players and surely one of its true legends. "I traveled everywhere. I went to Detroit. I went to Penn State. I was Syracuse's No. 1 fan because my kid was finally playing. I got to be like every other father. I got to sit in the seats and scream like crazy."

There was one evening, though, when Dolph did a teensy weensy bit more than sit in the seats...although he did, in fact, scream like crazy.

"Villanova," he said. "I already had the reputation of being a yeller, and I guess I deserved it. But that night I made a complete fool of myself. Even my wife was telling me, 'Shut up, you jerk.' But I didn't."

The date was February 17, 1981. The site was Philadelphia's Palestra, or as Dolph calls it, "that old bull ring"...and when Papa Schayes saw Danny foul out against the Wildcats, he responded the way Curly once did when he ran out of cheese.

"Villanova had a guy named John Pinone, who was a very good player," Dolph said. "He was about six-foot-five and smart as hell. When he'd get the ball, he'd back into Danny, create contact, shout 'Ooooh,' and shoot the ball. And this rookie referee called three or four fouls on Danny on that same exact play. So, as I'm watching this going on, I'm really getting furious.

"Finally, the ref fouled Danny out of the game, we lose (88-78), and for some stupid reason I rush the court. Brendan Malone, one of Boeheim's assistants, is charging the ref from one direction and I'm coming in from the other. And as we're closing in on him—and this is my story, and I'm sticking to it—I trip and kind of bump the ref. But when I saw it on tape later on, it looked like I was a bowling ball and the ref was a bowling pin."

In an instant, police officers were in the mix, breaking up the fracas, and the next thing Dolph knew, he was being led off the floor to boos and taunts and the kind of language that would wrinkle a pair of pants.

"So, it's the next morning," said Dolph. "And the *Philadelphia Daily News* comes out with this huge headline across the back page. 'Hall Of Shamer Attacks Referee.' I mean, it looked like the headline you'd use for the start of World War III. And on the front page, they lumped me in with a

Jack the Ripper copycat in England and a doctor who'd killed somebody. I mean it. Two murderers and me. Those were the big stories on Page One.

"So, we go to the airport...and wouldn't you know it? We're on the team's flight home to Syracuse. Well, you know, I'm trying to sneak around and not be noticed. But I'm six-foot-eight, so how am I going to do that? When the players saw me, they said to Danny, 'Hey, there's your father. He's Public Enemy No. 1.' Danny was kind of shunning me. You know, he was, like, 'I've got to get away from this idiot.' And I didn't blame him. The whole thing was one of the most embarrassing moments in my life."

That's right. There was at least one other. And that took place in the Miami Arena on May 4, 1997, during an NBA playoff series between the Orlando Magic and the Miami Heat.

"Danny was with the Magic then, and I was at the game along with about 30 other fans from Orlando," said Dolph. "And in the middle of the third quarter, the Miami mascot starts soaking us with water from one of those tommy-gun sprayers. Well, we're all getting wet, and I'm incensed.

"Now, you've to picture this: The mascot is a rabbit. A big rabbit. A big, big rabbit. Like, eight feet tall. So, I get up to tell him to knock it off. And I'm looking up and yelling at the rabbit head even though the guy's real head inside is in the middle of the rabbit's stomach. The next thing you know, I throw an elbow at the rabbit, and we're wrestling, and I'm grabbing for the tommy-gun."

Again, just like at the Palestra following the SU-Villanova game 16 years earlier, the police quickly arrived on the scene with every intent to haul Dolph—who was two weeks shy of his 70th birthday—off to the hoosegow.

"But I got saved," Dolph declared. "Everybody around

me was telling the cops, 'Leave him alone. He's just a senile old man.' So, they did. Meanwhile, I found out later that Rony Seikaly, another SU guy who was also with Orlando, saw what was happening, poked my son right there in the middle of the game and said, 'Look up there, Danny. Your father's at it again.'

"Oh, it was crazy. It really was. And you know what was really nuts? My grandchildren came up to me when I got home and asked, 'Hey, Grandpa. Why'd you beat up the bunny?"

Good question. After all, the bunny hadn't called a single foul on Danny.

JIM BOEHEIM'S SUDDENLY
SOGGY SENSATION

This just in: Jim Boeheim has a temper. He can get agitated. He can stomp and snort and blow like a noontime factory whistle. And while the long-time Syracuse basketball coach can appear positively beastly when he gets his veins and eyes bulging all at once, there are times when he can provide a bit of comic relief.

Even if it is unintended.

The date is December 10, 1980. The site is Michigan, where the 20th-ranked Orangemen are playing the University of Detroit. And the halftime mood inside the SU locker room is most foul. After all, the Syracuse athletes have used some foolish play just before the horn to give away much of the big lead they had erected...and they know that a thin slice of hell is about to be unleashed.

"I'd just popped open a can of Coke and Jimmy comes storming in," Leo Rautins recalled. "And he's all riled up. 'What are you guys doing? You're going to Illinois State from here and they're going to kill you!' I was sitting the closest to him and he's screaming about an inch from my face and he's spitting on me...and all of a sudden he grabs my arm and starts shaking it.

"Remember, I'd just opened that can of Coke. And I'm holding it in the arm Jimmy's shaking. And now, it starts to squirt. He's looking into my eyes and yelling, and all of a sudden you can tell he's starting to feel something. He doesn't want to look down, but he does want to look down, you know what I mean? And he keeps yelling, even though he knows something's not right.

"Well, Eddie Moss is sitting next to me, and he sees what's going on and he's trying to hold in his laughter so hard that he's all but peeing in his pants. And I can barely stop myself from laughing, too. Because the soda is spraying right into Boeheim's crotch. I'm telling you, that was funny."

The game, which the Orangemen would eventually win by a score of 93-79, was only the fourth in the Syracuse playing career of Rautins, who'd sat out the previous season after having transferred from Minnesota. And it more or less served as an omen, because the truth of the matter is that Boeheim and Rautins didn't get along all that well back then.

"Jimmy wanted me to play power forward, so I got heavier," said Rautins, a native of Toronto who's stayed in basketball as an NBA analyst for Canadian television. "My thing with him was, 'I'll play power forward and rebound and do those things for you, but I have to handle the ball for me. That's my game.' But I never really got in the flow and Jimmy never really had a lot of confidence in me, and we struggled with each other that first year. I honestly didn't know if I was going to stay at Syracuse."

Happily, the static eventually faded and the six-foot-eight Rautins morphed into a kind of freak, covering power forwards on defense, handling the ball on offense as a point guard of sorts...and eventually leading the Orangemen as a senior in the disparate categories of rebounding and assists. Indeed, Leo became so good at so much that he ended up as a first-round draft choice of the Philadelphia 76ers in 1983 and later spent six years as a well-paid professional in Italy, France and Spain.

But for a while there at SU, his basketball life was touch and go.

"We were a mishmash of a team while I was at Syracuse," said Rautins of his clubs that went 59-35 and to only one NCAA Tournament during his three seasons of eligibility. "We had a small forward [Tony Bruin] and a guard [Erich Santifer] who played around the basket, we had a point guard [Gene Waldron] who didn't like to handle the ball, we had an undersized center [six-foot-six Andre Hawkins], and we had me out on the perimeter. It's amazing that we did what we did when you think about. Because our teams were small and weird."

And they were often in the firing line of Jim Boeheim. But then, Jim Boeheim was once in the firing line of a can of Coke. Which only goes to show that things have a way of evening out.

Before "Bullet" Billy Gabor became an NBA All-Star as a Syracuse National, he was a Helms Foundation All-American as a Syracuse Orangeman.
The Post-Standard/Jon Olson

Some Syracuse club had to be the first to advance to the NCAA Tournament, and this 1957 outfit–with a starting five of Manny Breland, Gary Clark, Jon Cincebox, Jim Snyder and Vinnie Cohen...but without Jim Brown–was it.
The Post-Standard / Bob Johnston

Roy Danforth was always quick with a joke, but after leading the Orangemen to the 1975 Final Four, the funnyman proved he could coach, too.

The Post-Standard/John Dowling

Jimmy Lee, himself, will tell you that no list of great Syracuse shooters would be complete without his name near the very top.
The Post-Standard File Photo

If the subject was music rather than basketball, it could have been stated that the thin-thinner-thinnest Louis Orr was on hand to play the piano, not carry it.

The Post-Standard/Bill Tynan

Perhaps the greatest Orangeman never to have played in the NBA, Roosevelt Bouie was the soup to Louis Orr's sandwich.

The Post-Standard/David Lassman

Danny Schayes, the happy product of a fabulous gene pool, made his dad, Dolph, one proud papa.

The Post-Standard / John Berry

Everyone liked the Pearl—Dwayne Washington—except for the Boston
College Eagles, who were victimized by "The Shot."
The Post-Standard / Rob Crandall

Believe it or not, Derrick Coleman could not only rebound, block shots, score and snarl, he could smile, too.

The Post-Standard/Dennis Nett

Once upon a time, Jim Boeheim gazed upon Billy Owens and saw near-perfection; later, others gazed upon Carmelo Anthony and saw Billy Owens.
The Post-Standard / Tara McPharland

No Orangeman has scored more points or worn higher socks than Lawrence Moten, who always took the floor with an itchy finger and warm shins.
The Post-Standard / Harry DiOrio

He might have signed a $115-million contract with the NFL's Philadelphia Eagles, but once upon a time Donovan McNabb played basketball at SU for nothing at all.

The Post-Standard/Dennis Nett

Through the long winters, referee Tim Higgins and four-year starter Jason Hart became as familiar to Syracusans as shovels and snowbanks.
The Post-Standard / Stephen D. Cannerelli

He was in a Syracuse uniform for just one season, but Carmelo Anthony
smiled through most of it and delivered a national title.
The Post-Standard/Stephen D. Cannerelli

The championship magic woven by Jim Boeheim and Carmelo Anthony was such that the renowned Argentine artist Perez Celis reached for his brush.
Poster courtesy of Point of Contact / Painting by Perez Celis

The Final Four wins over Texas and Kansas in April of 2003 put the crown on Jim Boeheim's head...and never mind that it looked more like a big, loony hat.

The Post-Standard / John Berry

LEO RAUTINS BECOMES A LEGEND

It makes every Orange fan's short list of the most wondrous athletic competitions ever waged in the Carrier Dome, on the SU campus, in the city of Syracuse, or maybe anywhere, for that matter.

And according to Leo Rautins, the last of the many luminaries in that show, 100,000 folks must have been in attendance on March 7, 1981, to witness SU's epic 83-80 triple-overtime conquest of Villanova in the Big East Conference's championship game.

"You know how certain events take place and, as the years go by, everybody says they were there?" asked Rautins. "Well, that was one of those events. I can't tell you how many people have come up to me over the years and said, 'Oh, yeah. I was there.' It seems that everyone I've run into was at that game, you know what I mean?"

The truth is, on that glorious Saturday afternoon there were "only" 13,477 observers inside the Dome, which was in its first season as the Orangemen's home court and, therefore, still a curiosity. But those in the pews saw magnificence unfold before their very eyes.

"It was the longest game in the world," said Rautins, then a six-foot-eight sophomore who would score 16 points and grab 11 rebounds against the Wildcats. "It just kept going and going and going. Both teams could have won it in regulation. Both teams could have won it in any of the overtimes. And both teams had the feeling more than once that they'd lost it and were toast."

Still, despite the tumult, the 20-year-old Rautins had another pressing matter on his mind. And it had nothing to do with Villanova's defense, Rollie Massimino's sideline strategy, or the fact that the savvy Wildcats were in the process of shooting 70 percent from the floor after halftime.

"The thing is, that was the first day of Spring Break," said Rautins. "And the dorms were closing at 6 p.m. And, honest to God, that's what was on my mind as the game kept going on and on. I mean, I kept looking at Bernie Fine's watch during timeouts and I kept thinking, 'I've gotta get to my dorm. I've gotta get my stuff out of there before I get locked out.'

"Here we are, maybe playing the greatest game in Big East history, and all I can think about is, 'Man, we've got to get this game over with, so I can get to my dorm.' So, finally, as we're about to begin the third overtime, I said to Bernie, 'Bernie, the dorms close at six o'clock. What am I gonna do?' He couldn't believe that."

Perhaps it was that ticking clock that helped inspire Rautins to tip in Erich Santifer's missed jumper—and give the Orangemen (who were ultimately bound for the NIT and a final won-lost record of 22-12) an 82-80 lead—with three seconds left in the third OT. More likely, it was a matter of Leo merely sizing up the situation.

"The score was tied with about six or eight seconds to play," Rautins, a Canadian Olympian who'd become a 1,000-point career scorer for the Orange, recalled. "During the timeout, the play called was for me to in-bound the ball to Santifer and he'd get it back to me, because I was having a pretty good game. He got the ball, all right. But I knew as soon as Erich got it, it wasn't coming back to me. That's just a matter of knowing your teammates. So, after I passed it in to Santifer, I just went to the bucket and when he missed the jumper, I was there. It was just a matter of being in the right place at the right time."

The tip-in flat out made Rautins a star. More than that, it made him a near-instant Syracuse legend. And yet, the dirty little secret is this: He almost didn't play in SU's wins over Georgetown and Villanova during that particular Big East Tournament. Not after he'd injured his right knee in an on-court collision during the opener against St. John's.

"I spent the night of the St. John's game in the infirmary on campus, with my leg being iced every 30 minutes all night long," Rautins said. "So, I virtually didn't get any sleep at all. And after the Georgetown game the next day, it was more or less the same thing, because I was up all night again getting iced. So by the time we played Villanova, I was exhausted."

And, don't forget, Leo was carrying that mental burden, too. You know, the one about his dormitory room.

"It turns out, it was kind of stupid on my part," said Rautins, who was named the MVP of the Big East Tournament. "After all my worrying, I found out that somebody had called the security people and told them we were playing a game. Like, they didn't know, right? That whole deal was such a huge thing on my mind, and it ended up never being an issue. It's amazing what can go through your head during a game. Kind of dumb, huh?"

Well, yeah. But no matter. The tip-in fell through the net, the Orangemen won their championship and a lasting memory was crafted by the 100,000 who'd later swear that they were in the Dome that afternoon.

Leo Rautins, meanwhile, would be sleeping like a baby in just a few hours.

LATE STARTER...STRONG FINISHER

Although Danny Schayes started for just one season during the four years he played on the Syracuse University basketball team, he remains the lone Orangeman to have participated in 1,000 NBA games.

That's right. Danny Schayes—the six-foot-11 center who'd averaged merely 5.7 points and 4.2 rebounds during those freshman, sophomore and junior campaigns he spent as Roosevelt Bouie's caddy—makes up SU's list of one.

Not Dave Bing. Not Derrick Coleman. Not Billy Owens. Not Sherman Douglas. Not Dwayne Washington. Not Louis Orr. Not Rony Seikaly. Not John Wallace. Not Leo Rautins. Not any of those, or other, glorious Orangemen.

No, it was Danny Schayes, who graduated as a Rhodes Scholar candidate from Syracuse in 1981 and—on the strength of his senior-year averages of 14.6 points and 8.4 rebounds—soon thereafter became the No. 1 draft choice of the Utah Jazz.

To be exact, Danny played in 1,138 NBA games (plus 69 playoff contests) spread across 18 NBA seasons for seven different NBA franchises (Utah, Denver, Milwaukee, the Lakers, Phoenix, Miami and Orlando). Heck, even his dad— Dolph, the wondrous Hall of Fame forward—played in "only" 1,059 NBA games.

"The thing with Danny," said Dolph, as proud as a father could ever be, "is that he always made the players around him better. I don't care what team he was on or which players were on the floor. Danny always made everybody better."

And he did well for himself, too, scoring 8,780 NBA points, grabbing 5,671 NBA rebounds and cashing NBA checks worth tens of millions of dollars. All of which beats a sharp stick in the eye.

"When Danny was in college, I spent a lot of time grousing in the wings," said Dolph, who led the old Syracuse Nationals to the NBA title in 1955, four years before Danny was born. "I'll admit it. But I always thought he should have played more at SU."

Apparently, Hal Grossman, one of the college game's top officials, agreed. And an incident that occurred during Danny's sophomore season provided a hint of this.

Indeed, while working Syracuse's 100-74 blasting of Pittsburgh in Manley Field House on January. 6, 1979, Grossman called a fifth foul on Bouie, who—though very late in the game—was still on the floor for the Orangemen despite the blowout up there on the scoreboard.

Not surprisingly, Jim Boeheim, SU's third-year coach, disagreed with the call (and there's no need to stop the presses for that news), barking loudly about how disgraceful it was that Bouie, his starting center, had just been disqualified.

"Oh, come on, Jim," Grossman said to Boeheim. "You're up a ton. Give Danny Schayes a few minutes."

Considering that Danny was named an honorable mention All-American by the Associated Press following his senior campaign—and during that season grabbed a Carrier Dome record 23 rebounds against Georgetown—perhaps Dolph and Grossman were right.

But then, maybe the kid was just saving himself for the pros.

A MEMORABLE SHOT, A PEARL'S SHRUG

The shot has been witnessed by thousands. By tens of thousands. By hundreds of thousands, thanks to the wonders of VCRs and ESPN Classic. And all of those folks who've seen it won't soon forget its long arc through the Carrier Dome air and into the far basket.

But the guy who slung it on the night of January 21, 1984—the guy who broke Boston College's basketball heart with his desperate 45-foot toss from near halfcourt just before the final horn—just sort of shrugs. Still.

"Everywhere I go, every time I go out, I hear about that shot," said Dwayne 'Pearl' Washington nearly 20 years after his heave fell through the net. "One guy told me he was up, way up, in the Dome. Up near the third rail. And when I hit that shot, he jumped so high, he almost came down over the rail. I get those kinds of stories all the time.

"But for me, I don't think of it as the signature of my career. If you watch the games on TV, you know I'm not the first guy ever to hit a half-court shot to win a game. And, in reality, when you look at it, Boston College wasn't Georgetown or St. John's. It wasn't a big-time school. It was Boston College."

Sure, that's what the head says. But the heart? The heart has always been another matter. And the heart remembers that the Orangemen, 11-3 coming into that game with the Eagles, were being led by a divine freshman named Pearl, who'd merely been the most ballyhooed recruit in SU history. And so, the shot became forevermore The Shot, capital T and capital S.

Because Pearl Washington, in his 15th game in a Syracuse uniform, launched it. And he beat BC in the process, 75-73.

"Oh, man," said Rafael Addison, who was Washington's Orange teammate for three seasons. "Everybody loved Pearl. Traveling with him was like traveling with a rock star. He was known everywhere. But it was a funny thing with him. The public knew Pearl as this flamboyant guy, but we knew him as a shy kind of person. On the court, Pearl was a super hero; with us in the locker room, he was Clark Kent. The fans saw him as Superman; we saw him as the quiet reporter."

It turns out that that quiet reporter saved Addison's bacon against Boston College because it was Addison's man, Martin Clark, who had (1) scored the basket with four seconds to play that had tied the game at 73-73, and (2) stood at the free-throw line with the chance to win it with his foul shot. Which meant it was Addison among all those Orangemen who'd most fretted during those final ticks of the clock.

"When Pearl hit that shot, I jumped higher than I've ever jumped in my life," said Addison, who scored 19 points that evening. "Believe me, I was happier than anybody in the building. Coach Boeheim came up to me in the locker room after the game and told me, 'You better thank your buddy, Pearl. He bailed you out.' And he wasn't playing around."

Simply, a landmark had been established that evening before a Dome house of 30,293. And a non-erasable memory had been created. There was the fabulous Pearl Washington, the Brooklyn kid who'd been dubbed by Boeheim the most important player he'd ever brought to town. And there was the ball sailing...sailing...sailing...

And then, splash! And it was as if Lindbergh had touched down in France all over again.

"Somebody from BC missed the free throw there at the end," recalled Washington, who was eight-for-10 from the field that night and scored a team-high 20 points. "And when he missed it, Sean Kerins got the rebound and passed it to me, and off I went. When I got to halfcourt, I just threw it up into the air. I could tell it was right on line. I just didn't know if it was going to be too short or too long. That's how those things usually are. You just don't know. And it went right in.

"After I let it go, I just kept running. I ran right off the floor. Didn't stop. When you get a whole lot of people charging the court—and I know a whole lot of people charged the court after that one—you don't want to take a chance on getting hurt. So running straight into the locker room I thought was the best thing to do."

And when he got there?

"I just enjoyed myself," Pearl said. "And I called my mother to tell her what happened."

Magic had happened, followed by happy mayhem. The Pearl had solidified himself as a jewel.

WE'D HEARD THE CHANT BEFORE

It started as a rumble, grew to a roar and finally became a thunder that nearly buckled the walls of the Carrier Dome.

"One more year! One more year! One more year!"

The throaty crowd of 33,071—the largest, on-campus, single-game gathering in NCAA basketball history—was pleading with Carmelo Anthony, the freshman star who was surely headed out the door and onto the NBA where all those wheelbarrows filled with money were waiting. Seemingly every man, woman and child who'd squeezed into the joint on that afternoon of March 9, 2003, was standing and very nearly begging. Loudly.

As the Orangemen knocked off poor Rutgers, however, in what had been unofficially billed as Anthony's last-ever college game in Syracuse, the whole scene seemed to have an air of deja vu about it. Because the Dome had seen this before. On March 16, 1986, as a matter of fact, when Dwayne "Pearl" Washington was serenaded with the same three words.

"One more year! One more year! One more year!"

"I thought it was nice that the fans were cheering for me," recalled Washington months after Anthony chose to prance off to the pros. "But I really didn't understand it. One more year? I wasn't going anywhere."

The occasion was the Orangemen's second-round NCAA Tournament contest with Navy, a heavy underdog that SU had whacked by 22 points on the same floor some 13 weeks earlier. But the ninth-ranked Syracuse club came out wholly overconfident and the Midshipmen's David Robinson was a colossus...and the Orangemen were crushed, 97-85.

"That was hard," Washington said. "That was tough. We just kind of thought we were going to win. We all did because we beat them so bad before. And then, David Robinson put a royal butt-kicking on us. I mean, he killed us."

Robinson, who was destined for the NBA himself, scored 35 points that day. And grabbed 11 rebounds. And blocked seven shots. The result was that the folks in the seats—without a competitive game to follow—were left to try to convince the fabulous Pearl, then a junior with career averages of 15.7 points and 6.7 assists per game, to put the NBA on hold.

Oh, how they'd taken to him over the years. To his creativity. To his big shots, lofted and made. To his grit.

On that latter point, he was the six-foot-two sophomore sprite who'd had enough of the brutish, seven-foot Patrick Ewing and had darn near knocked the Georgetown giant down in the 1985 Big East Tournament at Madison Square Garden. And who could possibly have forgotten that?

"Ewing was one of those guys we didn't like," Washington said. "But it wasn't just him. It was the whole Georgetown team. That day he bullied Andre Hawkins. So, on the next play downcourt, I elbowed Ewing right in the stomach and he doubled over. And then he came up swinging. He missed and everybody came between us right away, and that was good because that way neither of us got thrown out of the game.

"You've got to remember, you're talking Patrick Ewing back then. And Pearl Washington back then. It was the Big East Tournament. It was the Garden. It didn't matter how big he was; I had to do what I had to do. I mean, Ewing had been 'doing us' the whole time I was in college and I was just tired of it."

It turned out to be the Pearl's last great stand because nine days later, Robinson and his Middies came to the Dome and swabbed the floor with the Orangemen. And by the end of the afternoon, they'd left the masses with but one choice: to chant at Pearl as they would at Anthony 17 years later.

"One more year! One more year! One more year!"

"You know what happened?" Washington admitted. "I looked around and thought that we just didn't have enough talent to get to the next level, which was the national championship game. We just didn't have it, so I decided to go to the pros.

"Now, looking back, I realize they went to the Final Four the very next season when I would have been a senior. Because they had Derrick Coleman, which I didn't know at the time. I'll never forget that night when they played Indiana in the championship game. I remember watching it on TV."

The Pearl, an NBA rookie who'd been stripped by the pros of much of his wizardry, was on the road somewhere with his new club, the New Jersey Nets. And he was thinking, at least for that night, how things might have been different had he listened to those howling Domers the previous March.

"One more year! One more year! One more year!"

It had been a nice thought.

ADDISON LOVES 'CUSE (WOOF, WOOF)

It's not just the fans who bleed orange. The players do, too. A fair amount of them, anyway. And among that group is Rafael Addison, who has forever looked upon his school the way those old Texicans did the Alamo.

"You know how we've all got something very important in our lives that's hidden deep inside of us?" asked Addison. "For me, that's Syracuse. Syracuse sculpted me. It pointed me in the right direction in life. Nobody can ever talk bad to me about Syracuse or my guys. Derrick Coleman...Pearl...any of them. I'll defend them all forever."

Raf is hopelessly devoted, all right. He has a Golden Retriever named Cuse. His New Jersey real estate company is called Cuse Corporation. He has both "Cuse" and "12" (his SU uniform number) in his e-mail address. And when the Orangemen upset North Carolina in the 1987 NCAA Tournament, Addison—then, a bold rookie with the Phoenix Suns—hung his old SU jacket in the cubicle of Walter Davis, the former Tar Heel-turned-Phoenix star who quickly (and angrily) threw it onto the clubhouse floor.

"I've become," Raf admitted, "a Syracuse fanatic."

Simply, he's been conditioned to be. Indeed, Addison left SU as a second-round draft choice of the Suns in 1986. And he proceeded to play for four teams in six NBA seasons before landing in Europe for a spell. And he's the head basketball coach at his old high school, Snyder High, in Jersey City. But no matter. Rafael Addison—who scored 1,876 points for SU between 1982-83 and 1985-86, and received some kind of All-American recognition as a sophomore, junior and senior—will forever be an Orangeman.

"I took my high school team up to Syracuse this past season," said Addison, referring to a 2002 Christmas tournament in which the orange-clad (what else?) Tigers participated. "And we were eating at a Denny's. And a couple finished their meal, walked by my table and said, 'Raf Addison! How you doing?' And my kids were, like, 'Coach, they still remember you up here? After all these years?' And I told them, 'Uh huh.' They couldn't believe it.

"But that's the way it is. I was in Home Depot yesterday and a guy said, 'You're Raf Addison. You played at Syracuse.' I got three telephone calls just today from people who saw me on ESPN Classic. That kind of stuff is always happening. And I haven't suited up for the Orangemen since 1986."

You know the old line about asking some chatty person for the time, and he or she ends up telling you how to build a watch? Well, that's kind of like Rafael Addison, who, as a high-school kid, flipped on Channel 9 one day at home, watched SU play in the 1981 NIT and all but decided on the spot to attend the university—hook, line and sinker.

Absolutely, this fellow loves his Orangemen. And he loves Jim Boeheim, even if he almost got hit by a locker-room stool tossed by the fiery coach midway through a halftime of hell and brimstone during the Marquette game in 1985.

"That was all right," said Addison, who started, as a six-foot-seven forward, in each of his final 95 games at SU. "He's just an intense man. I remember we were playing cards in Greece on our overseas trip before my senior year. It was me and Coach and Bernie Fine and Derek Brower. We were playing 'Spades.'

"I guess I was talking a lot. I guess I was talking too much for Coach. To be honest about it, I was talking some real junk and he didn't take it well. He told me to be quiet. And I got to thinking, 'Whoa, this guy is competitive.' I mean, it was just a card game. 'You're not winning,' he told me. 'Just deal.' In the end, I want to say I won. But I can't. Coach won."

Even before that, however, Boeheim had won an unwavering loyalty. And according to Rafael Addison, who sells Syracuse basketball the way Prof. Harold Hill once sold boys marching bands, Boeheim continues to do so.

"We're the one program in the nation with the same coach for all these years," Addison said. "When you come around, you always feel welcome. All these other schools have new coaches all the time, so when the old guys come back, they don't feel at home. They don't feel wanted. Me, I'll always be part of it. I'll always be part of Syracuse."

And for proof of Raf's devotion, there is this: If his dog, Cuse, should ever get a little brother dog, his name would likely be B.B.

"Yeah, B.B.," Addison said. "That would stand for Boeheim and Bernie. They've been up there for a long, long time. They're like M&Ms. Some day, they'll be naming a candy after those guys."

And Rafael Addison will happily push it door to door.

"I'LL TAKE PEARL AND
CHRIS WASHBURN"

It was early in Syracuse University's 1986 football season, the one that began with four consecutive defeats, three of which took place inside the Carrier Dome. And Jim Boeheim, the basketball coach—and avowed Orange football fan—was a tad agitated on a Saturday afternoon in the Dome's pressbox.

His feistiness, mind you, had nothing to do with the SU football team, which was losing down there on the carpeted field below. Nah, Boeheim was a bit peeved because a local sportswriter had suggested that the New Jersey Nets might someday wish that they hadn't chosen the six-foot-two Dwayne Washington with the NBA draft's 13th overall selection a few months earlier.

"I'm telling you," Boeheim said, "Pearl is going to end up being the best pick in that draft."

"I don't think so," the local sportswriter said. "He was terrific in college, no question about that. But I don't know if he necessarily translates to the pro game."

This, of course, was dangerous business. Boeheim, a voracious reader, was clearly more intelligent than the local sportswriter. And Boeheim, who was about to enter his 11th campaign as SU's head coach, had devoted the bulk of his life to observing basketball. So, this seemed to be an argumentative mismatch on the order of Reagan vs. Mondale.

But the local sportswriter, who'd covered the NBA in an earlier incarnation, wouldn't budge. This, even if there were those who believed that Boeheim, should he have chosen such a career path, would have made for a dandy NBA personnel man.

"If not Pearl," said the forever-loyal Boeheim, referring to the former Orange sensation, "who do you think is going to have the better career?"

"I've got two guys in mind," said the local sportswriter. "I like Chuck Person (drafted No. 4) and Ron Harper (drafted No. 8). I can't decide between the two."

"OK, fine," said Boeheim. "You take those guys. I'll take Pearl and Chris Washburn (drafted No. 3). And down the road we'll see who's right."

Well, we're down the road. Way, way down the road. And all four of those 1986 draftees have long since retired. And so, it's time to look at the numbers.

Washington, who left Syracuse following his junior campaign, and Washburn, the troubled kid out of North Carolina State? They combined to score 1,882 points in 266 games spread across five NBA seasons. Auburn's Person and Harper, from Miami of Ohio? They combined to score 27,768 points in 1,952 games spread across 29 NBA seasons. Oh, and they finished 1-2 in the Rookie of the Year voting, too, in 1987.

Slam dunk for the local sportswriter? Sure, but he hasn't been able to gloat terribly much because that 1986 NBA Draft had also been dotted with the likes of Brad Daugherty, Jeff Hornacek, Dennis Rodman, Arvidas Sabonis, Mark Price, Dell Curry and John Salley. And he didn't consider any of them.

But then, neither did Boeheim.

DERRICK COLEMAN, THE GOOD GUY

Larry Kimball, SU's Sports Information Director Emeritus, came to Syracuse in 1966 and has never left. And in all that time, he's dealt with Orangeman after Orangeman after Orangeman. Tall or small, skinny or fat, friendly or sour—it didn't matter. If you were a Syracuse athlete, sooner or later you had to do business with Kimball, a member of the CoSIDA Hall of Fame and a fellow with some serious perspective.

So, when Larry insists that Derrick Coleman—dismissed by so many as the north end of a southbound horse—is a good guy, maybe we should believe him.

"I don't like to talk about favorites," Kimball said. "That's not fair to all the people I've dealt with. But Derrick is one of my all-time favorites."

Certainly, nobody could ever take issue with Coleman's formidable basketball skills. After all, during his four-year Orange career, he averaged 15.0 points, 10.7 rebounds, 2.2 blocks and 1.3 steals per game while leading his Syracuse clubs to a cumulative record of 113-31 and to the NCAA title affair in 1987.

And soon thereafter, Coleman became (for a little while, anyway) the highest-paid athlete in the history of the NBA.

But the notion that Derrick—known as much for his moodiness as his rebounding—could make anybody's list of "all-time favorites" is man-bites-dog news.

"He was a funny kid," Kimball said. "He had all these chip-on-the-shoulder things going on, but he'd come into my office and...well, you know how Carmelo Anthony has that great smile? I'm telling you, Derrick could also melt you with his. It's just that when he went before the public, his persona would make things very difficult."

Truth be told, Coleman—an equal-opportunity crank—could also frustrate Kimball, one of his greatest champions.

"He hated to do those postgame press conferences," Kimball said. "I remember when we beat Virginia in the NCAA Tournament in 1990 in Richmond to move onto the Regional in New Orleans. Well, Derrick wouldn't go to the press conference. He just wouldn't. He just sat there, shaking his head.

"So, I begged him. I told him, 'Derrick, for God's sake, you just won. Enjoy yourself. Go to the press conference, please.' So, he gets up and he throws his arm around me and he says, 'For you, Mr. K, I'll go.' And when he got there in front of the microphones, he was as charming as could be.

"I have one of those 11-by-14 pictures that he gave to me before he left us. And he wrote on it, 'To Mr. K, who made me an All-American.' I'm telling you, I have very pleasant memories of that guy. I really do."

Oh, and there was this, too, about Coleman: For all of his celebrated churlishness, he was largely devoid of ego.

"When he decided to come back for his senior year and not move on to the NBA," Kimball recalled, "Derrick came into my office, sat down and said, 'I'm staying.' And that was it. 'I'm staying.' Nothing more to it than that. Today, you'd have 10,000 cameras and microphones and the whole big deal.

"But not Derrick. 'I'm staying.' That was it. Period. Kind of amazing, huh?"

1987 FINAL FOUR:
SQUINT AND YOU'LL SEE 2003

He'd watched them through so much of the season as they won...and won...and won...and woke up at the Final Four in New Orleans. And then it dawned on Howard Triche, who'd always figured deja vu was a French pastry or something.

He'd seen this before. No, that wasn't right. He'd *lived* it in an earlier life. The youth, the exuberance, the wonderment of it all. Yeah, Howard Triche looked at those 2002-03 Orangemen and he saw only familiar faces from the 1986-87 campaign.

Anthony, the stunning freshman...Derrick Coleman, the stunning freshman. Gerry McNamara, the spunky freshman guard...Sherman Douglas, the spunky sophomore guard. Kueth Duany, the steady senior hand in the backcourt...Greg Monroe, the steady senior hand in the backcourt. Hakim Warrick, the high-flying sophomore...Stephen Thompson, the high-flying freshman. Craig Forth, the earnest sophomore center...Rony Seikaly, the earnest junior center.

"When you look at it," said Triche, "the guys who went to the Final Four this year ['03] and us [in '87] were pretty much alike. We were both real young and we both kind of went along with Syracuse basketball tradition because, you know, in general, when expectations aren't that high, the teams usually do well.

"You've got to remember that Sherman didn't play all that much the year before. And Derrick and Stevie were freshmen. And Rony was kind of up and down. And it wasn't like Greg and I were heralded players who were going to carry the team. I mean, when we started out, who knew much about us as a team? You could say the same about Carmelo and those guys. And both of us made it to the Final Four."

In Louisiana, separated by 16 years. At the Superdome, where they were both underdogs playing for the crown against a college basketball monstrosity, either Indiana or Kansas. Before ranting crowds that were, in size, somewhere between the total populations of upstate New York cities Binghamton and Schenectady.

And it was all so spectacular, right down to the opponent's shots at the end on each of those magnificent Monday nights—the one by the Hoosiers' Keith Smart that bottomed out after clearing Triche's outstretched hand in '87; and the one by the Jayhawks' Michael Lee that didn't after being blocked by Warrick into the seats in '03.

"Neither team started out with real, known talent," said Triche. "But for each team, the talent came alive during the season."

Triche could be considered the best of all spokesmen for those two Orange carpet rides to the Final Four. A native of Syracuse and a graduate of Corcoran High School, he was an Orange senior in '87 who would evolve into a married father of two and a training manager at the Anheuser-Busch plant in nearby Baldwinsville, N.Y., by the time Anthony showed up on the SU campus.

So, with Coleman and Douglas and Seikaly and Monroe and all those others having left town—and with Anthony and Duany out the door—Triche remains the residing link between the two clubs. Moreover, he lives on as the co-poster boy of that famous 1987 title affair that produced Bobby Knight's third national championship.

Uh huh. As every newsreel clearly shows, there was Indiana's Smart, rising from the floor, 16 feet from the basket with some four seconds to play...and there was SU's Triche, the closest Orangeman to him. And in an instant, what had been a 73-72 Syracuse lead became a 74-73 Hoosiers victory. And, oh, despair wrapped itself around SU's stunned athletes—whose NCAA Tournament run had included wins over Georgia Southern, Western Kentucky, Florida, North Carolina and Providence—like a heavy, wet rope.

"When that shot went in, it was like somebody ripped my heart out," said Triche, a six-foot-five forward, who, at the time, had only recently recovered from a severe case of the flu. "It was shock. It was disbelief. It was, like, 'OK, what now?' I remember in the locker room, things were pretty dismal. Coach Boeheim couldn't say anything. He just couldn't. You ended up asking yourself, 'Did this really happen?'"

Until then, of course—before Smart found the Orangemen's chest with his stake—it had been magical. Syracuse led the regal Hoosiers, 52-44, with 12 1/2 minutes to play. IU's Steve Alford, who'd scored 19 of his 23 points in the first 29 minutes, was in the process of flat-lining, and the SU devotees in the massive Dome house of 64,959 were thundering.

"It was all pretty spectacular," said Triche, who'd thought of transferring from Syracuse following his sophomore season, but stuck around and started as both a junior and senior. "The thing I'll never forget was being at the foul line for free throws. You'd be standing there, and you'd be looking at yourself because the big video screen was right behind the backboard. I mean, when you think about it, that's quite a distraction."

Keith Smart, though, made it all disappear. And in the process, he made Howard Triche—thanks to those never-ending ESPN Classic replays—an Orangeman for the ages.

"Most people who know basketball know what happened," said Triche. "It's been kind of portrayed that it was all my fault, but I just happened to be there. We were playing a box-and-one or something, and I was out on top. All I know is that the ball went inside [to Indiana's Daryl Thomas] and I doubled down to help Rony, and then it got kicked out to Keith.

"He apparently wasn't supposed to be a jump shooter, and he took the shot really quick. All I could do was contest it. I wasn't really trying to block it because I wasn't close enough. If you look, I just kind of made a circle with my hands. It was kind of a wave. The way the photos and some TV angles made it look, I was right there. But I wasn't. I was a long ways away."

Alas, the thing found string, and except for a last-second heave by the Orangemen—a pass that was intercepted—it was over. Douglas's 20 points? Coleman's 19 rebounds? Seikaly's double-double of 18 points and 10 rebounds? Triche's eight points? None of it was enough. Not on the night when Keith Smart, who would finish with 21 points (including 12 of IU's last 15) became a Final Four legend, an Indiana immortal and Syracuse's own Freddy Krueger.

"Bobby Knight gave a lot of credit to Alford," Triche said. "But it was Smart who killed us. In the second half, especially, he played like a man possessed."

And a man out of reach of Triche, who was just too far away to become the Hakim Warrick of his time.

Still...

"I think we had a great run," Triche said of that SU bunch that went 31-7. "It was a great year. If it wasn't for that last shot, we'd have been like Carmelo and those guys."

Yeah, that last shot. The one that will forever jolt Howard's sense of deja vu. The one that just won't go away.

"When do people bring it up?" asked Triche, 16 years after Smart splashed from the side. "All the time. That's all. Just all the time."

HE WAS STILL SMARTING

When the Orangemen defeated Oklahoma in Albany's 2003 East Regional to advance to the Final Four in New Orleans, they set off the predictable wave of joy throughout central and upstate New York. But they were also made to feel once again the ghostly cold breath of Indiana's Keith Smart on their collars.

You remember Keith Smart. You remember how his 16-foot jumper along the left baseline had been the bolo punch that found SU's chin in those final precious seconds of the 1987 title game in the Louisiana Superdome. You remember how the Orangemen seemed so stunned by Smart's swish that they apparently hesitated before calling a timeout.

Yeah, you remember Keith Smart, who became the Hoosiers' signature in their 74-73 triumph that painful night. And Syracuse coach Jim Boeheim remembered him, too, although in the days leading up to the Orangemen's return to New Orleans, he basically tried to deny it.

"I don't look back," Boeheim said.

It was a nice try, but nobody was buying such silliness. Of course, he'd looked back and he'd seen Smart each time. Why, Boeheim admitted as much when he declared after his club had knocked off Kansas for his first NCAA Tournament title that the image of Smart had haunted him in each of the previous 16 years.

Moreover, the SU pooh-bah all but confessed to looking back when, on the day before the magnificent '03 affair with the Jayhawks, he was asked to clarify once and for all what had happened in those dazed moments after Smart had found the net with his prayer in '87.

Did his Orangemen freeze? Had they panicked and forgotten how much time remained on the clock? How might college basketball history have been changed if somebody in a Syracuse uniform—anybody in a Syracuse uniform—had been quicker to react?

And Boeheim—who doesn't look back (wink, wink) and hadn't ever reflected on Smart and his shot (wink, wink)—paused not at all before responding.

"The ball went in the basket," he said, "when it was just below '4,' and it actually went to '3' and everybody said we didn't get a timeout. We got it with '2' (although newspaper reports put the number at '1') and it was our last timeout. If we could have gotten it with '3' or '4,' it wouldn't have made any difference We were going to do the same thing.

"We ran a long play, a long pass play, which is what we would have run. They stole the ball. It wouldn't have mattered if it was 3, 4, 5, or 6 left. We would have run the same thing. If we had two timeouts left, then it would have made a difference.

"At the end of the Georgia game in the 1996 Tournament, there were five seconds left and we had two timeouts, so we threw the ball to halfcourt, called time out and were able to run a good play (and eliminate the Bulldogs, 83-81, in overtime). But we didn't have two timeouts against Indiana, so it didn't make any difference. The clock would have run out. We would have run the same play."

So, there. The Orangemen's milling around hadn't caused serious damage to the cause back there in 1987. No, Keith Smart and only Keith Smart had been the reason for the heartbreak.

Sixteen years later, that was Jim Boeheim's story. And he was sticking to it.

THE ORANGE FOREIGN LEGION

When Carmelo Anthony was chosen by the Denver Nuggets with the third pick in the 2003 NBA Draft, he became the 47th Syracuse University basketball player—dating back to Bob Savage in 1950—to be selected by the likes of the Knicks and the Jazz, the Pistons and the Kings, the Nets and the Clippers, and all those other NBA teams.

But through the years, the Orangemen haven't just dribbled along those glamorous NBA floors; they've also headed overseas where so many foreigners have been only too happy to sneak a peek at what SU fans have saluted for all this time.

Why, in the very season of Syracuse's first NCAA Tournament championship, 11 different Orangemen were listed on professional rosters on the other side of the Atlantic. They were, alphabetically, Adrian Autry (Italy), Ryan Blackwell (England), Todd Burgan (Lebanon), Ethan Cole (Norway), LeRon Ellis (Italy), Jason Hart (Greece), Michael Lloyd (Israel), Lawrence Moten (Greece), Elvir Ovcina (Germany), J.B. Reafsnyder (Belgium) and Preston Shumpert (France).

So, the SU basketball gospel has spread to distant shores, and it is in good hands. But seeds had to have been sown, and two of the earliest sowers were Dale Shackleford and Herman Harried, who were once Syracuse Orangemen but ended up being Worthing Bears.

Yeah, Worthing Bears, playing an hour or so south of London in the National League of England's Second Division. And they did so for about $20,000 apiece—excluding their free car, free lodging, free heat, free electricity and free beer.

"It's great," Shackleford said at the time, which was during the 1989-90 season. "We own the town. If the time is right, we get free lunches. See that sporting goods store over there? Herman goes in there all the time and the guys give him stuff for nothing. Sneakers. Things like that."

Well, why not? The six-foot-seven Harried, who was good for 2.4 points and 2.1 rebounds per game in his Orange career that ended in 1989, had become a monster in England where he averaged some 30 points and 18 rebounds each night for the Bears. Yeah, Herman Harried.

"Herman is, without question, the best player in England," Colin Smith, one of the Worthing club's four directors, said back in 1990. "And he's definitely the greatest player at his position our league has seen in five years."

And the six-foot-six Shackleford, who'd averaged 12.1 points and 7.3 rebounds between 1975-79 while at SU? *The Worthing Herald* apparently believed he could not merely hit jumpers from hither (never mind yon), but change water into wine. Which is understandable, of course, when you consider that Dale once registered 53 triple-doubles in a row for the Bears.

"Dale Shackleford," read the newspaper's account of the Bears' 103-82 conquest of the Hemel Royals in 1989, "gave a performance of basketball mastery, scintillating in its total dominance, control, execution, vision and artistic brilliance, to preserve the Bears' unbeaten home record."

Funny, huh? Once embraced as Orangemen, Herman and Shack—respected, revered...reinvented—experienced a bit of deja vu as Bears. As Worthing Bears, hard by the English Channel. But with a British twist.

"You walk around these old people and they kind of gawk at you," Harried said once upon a time. "They're not accustomed to tall guys. They're amazed. You walk by and you hear, 'Wow. Did you see him?' You get little kids grabbing their parents and saying, 'Are they real?' It's kind of strange."

The upshot? Harried and Shackleford might just as well have said to Toto, "We're not in Syracuse anymore." But then, a whole bunch of other Orangemen, who've discovered through the years that the world isn't so big a place, could have told that little dog the same thing.

CALIFORNIA'S IMPORTS

It's crazy. That's what it is. Absolutely nuts.

Why would a guy from California, where the sun hangs high in a cloudless sky and where the girls are not always fully clothed, leave the easy living behind and enlist with the Orangemen? Why, indeed, would he head for central New York, complete with its sleet, dankness and bundled-up coeds? Why would he trade the breezy Santa Monica Pier for wintry Marshall Street?

"Are you kidding?" said Mike Hopkins. "I loved doing all of that. It was, like, the best thing ever."

He wasn't the first or the last Californian to sign on with SU. Stephen Thompson and Erik Rogers began the parade in 1986. And Earl Duncan followed in 1987. And Richard Manning arrived in 1988. And LeRon Ellis came in 1989. And Scott McCorkle descended in 1990. And Jason Hart showed up in 1996. And Tony Bland materialized in 1998.

But Mike Hopkins—who passed on the likes of Pepperdine, Long Beach State, and the University of San Diego to join the Orangemen out of Mater Dei High School in Laguna Hills in 1989—has long been considered SU's California posterboy.

"When I was growing up, I'd leave the house on Saturdays and Sundays at six in the morning and be on the water all day," said Hopkins, who favored T Street Beach in San Clemente. "I'd camp out there with my friends and with the families of my friends. It was awesome."

And yet, Hopkins willingly left it all in his rear-view mirror—the surf, the sand, the tan lines, the bikinis—for Syracuse, where between Halloween and Mother's Day the sun reveals itself only on whim. Which once more begs the question: Why?

"Those were the years when all the games were on CBS," Hopkins said. "The exposure of the Big East was exploding. It was the highest level of college basketball. And I loved Pearl Washington. He was my idol. And another thing. All of the players are, like, superstars all over the campus. So, being a superstar and playing for a Top 10 team nationally...I mean, how do you beat that? I wanted to be a part of it. The bad weather didn't affect me at all. The winter was never really an issue."

He did, however, prepare for it—as all California kids must.

"I just remember acting as if I was going off to Antarctica," said Hopkins, who became one of Jim Boeheim's assistant coaches in 1995. "I didn't know what to expect, so I showed up with those big, funny Sorrell boots. And I had a jacket that would have made the Abominable Snowman jealous. And long underwear. I'd never worn long underwear. But I had long underwear. My first day of class, it took me 25 minutes to undress before I could sit down."

He adapted, though, and became not only one of the Orangemen's most popular players in history, but a pretty good one, too. Hopkins started as a six-foot-five guard for two years, became team captain as a senior and averaged 5.7 points (including 9.2 during his final season in 1992-93) in the 111 games in which he played.

And look at him now. Fifteen years after leaving the zephyrs of Southern California for the cold winds of central New York, he was still in Syracuse—and he was still loving it.

"Don't get me wrong," said Hopkins, who did take a break from the Orange scene to play pro ball for a couple of seasons in the CBA and Europe. "There are some days when things aren't going well and it's gray outside and you look out the window and say, 'Whoa.' You know about the big suicide rate in Seattle with all of that rain out there, don't you? Well...

"You know, people out there try to bash you in recruiting. 'It's cold up there. Why go to Syracuse?' But if you're a basketball player, weather is not a big deal. You're on the road. You're playing. You're busy. You don't have time to think about it. If you love to play basketball, this is the greatest place in the world. I used to tell Jason Hart all the time, 'It's warm in the Dome.' And it is."

Not as warm as T Street Beach, sure. But then, those surfer boys (and girls) have never heard the roar of 30,000 fans, either. Mike Hopkins will tell you that'll take the chill off.

HE WAS CARMELO BEFORE CARMELO

More than a decade prior to his actual arrival in Syracuse, there had been a virtual sighting in an Orange uniform of Carmelo Anthony. And, in retrospect, it turned out to be a happily eerie one.

Like Anthony, this pre-Carmelo was a six-foot-eight Swiss Army knife with nostrils. He could do it all—from near, from far and from every place in between—on the court and was destined to be the No. 3 pick in the NBA Draft. And, importantly, none of the national huzzahs he'd inspired while in high school had resulted in a head that had outgrown his hat.

Oh, yeah. Carmelo Anthony was fabulous in his one and only year at SU. But he really wasn't a whole lot better than Billy Owens had been in the 1990-91 campaign, during which he nearly became a basketball Mona Lisa.

"Watching Billy Owens play basketball, and coaching him, is a privilege that only one coach gets to do," said Jim Boeheim as that campaign unfolded. "I get satisfaction in life from my daughter and from watching guys approach perfection playing basketball. So, some day down the road, I'll look back on this season and say, 'That was the year I had Billy Owens. He reached towards perfection in basketball.' That might be the only thing I remember, no matter what happens."

How good was Billy Owens as a junior, his final year in a Syracuse uniform? One could argue that during that campaign he crafted as spectacular an individual season as any other Orangeman ever has. And he did it, too, for a wonderful team that went 26-6 and ascended to as high as No. 3 in the polls.

He averaged 23.3 points (the fourth highest such SU number since World War II), 11.6 rebounds (the second highest such SU number in the near 30 years between 1975-2003) and 3.5 assists (with Adrian Autry in the backcourt). He shot 50.9 percent from the field, collected a combined 115 blocks and steals, and delivered 19 double-doubles in 32 games.

He had games of 36 points and 14 rebounds vs. Boston College, of 33 and 16 vs. Pittsburgh, of 31 and 10 vs. Notre Dame, of 30 and 12 again vs. Boston College, of 28 and 14 vs. St. John's, of 28 and 13 vs. Indiana, of 25 and 16 vs. Providence, of 24 and 13 vs. Seton Hall, of 21 and 12 vs. North Carolina State. And so on and so forth.

Ah, but as his Orangemen went only 5-3 in three NCAA tournaments—bowing to Illinois (1989), Minnesota (1990) and Richmond (1991) along the way—what Owens didn't do was bask in a national championship glow. And that is where the disconnect with Anthony begins.

But barely. You can't actually be perfect, you know. And you can't really be a basketball Mona Lisa. But Jim Boeheim, who will talk with reverence some day down the road when he discusses Billy Owens, will say that he had at least one player who came close.

ONE GOOD DEED DESERVES ANOTHER

Here's the deal: You offer a small kindness to Jim Boeheim; he'll provide a subtle favor in return. And for Exhibit "A," there was the exchange of courtesies between the Orange basketball coach and the family Osier of Fayetteville, N.Y.

It began with SU's melodramatic affair at the Carrier Dome with the undermanned Princeton Tigers on December 17, 1994. And it ended nearly six years later on a gorgeous summer afternoon during Pearl Washington's Coaches vs. Cancer Golf Tournament at Green View Country Club in West Monroe, N.Y.

The game? Oh, the 16th-ranked Orangemen won, 67-65...but only after surviving a trio of three-point baskets buried by the Tigers' Jason Osier, a reserve sophomore guard out of Fayetteville-Manlius High School, located some five miles as the crow flies from the Dome. The last of those, by the way, was buried from the top of the key with 31 seconds remaining in regulation and sent the contest into overtime at 54-54.

It was in that extra session that Boeheim received his friendly token from the sizzling Osier, the local boy who—while wide open on the far side of the three-point arc—shouted to his Princeton teammate, Sydney Johnson, in the final seconds of OT. Apparently, though, Jason didn't shout loudly enough because Johnson took the potential game-winner himself. And missed it.

Fast-forwarding nearly six years, Boeheim found himself playing in Pearl's golf tournament with Ken Osier, Jason's father and a fellow who was in the midst of one of his infamous "one-under" rounds. Which is to suggest that poor

Ken was one under a bush, one under a tree, one under a ball-washer all day long. And he never did come out of his funk.

So, Boeheim, the former Syracuse golf coach who was perhaps remembering Jason's benevolence for not having shouted loudly enough back in '94, repaid the family Osier with some ever-helpful advice that had nothing to do with the banalities of driving, chipping and putting.

"I think," he told the elder Osier after Ken had staggered from the course, "you should take two weeks off. Then, quit."

Hey, you scratch Jim Boeheim's back. He'll scratch yours.

THE GUY WITH THE
POINTS AND THE SOCKS

The scorers, all kinds of scorers, have passed through now for years, for decades, from one century into the next. They've been long and short...beefy and lean...from overseas and from just down the street. And since 1901, they've relentlessly put the ball in the basket.

One, though, has to be at the top of that list. Just one out of all those Dave Bings and Sherman Douglases and Derrick Colemans and Billy Gabors and Stephen Thompsons and Bill Smiths and Rudy Hacketts and Vinnie Cohens and all the rest.

One. And only one. And his name is Lawrence Moten, who went about his loud statistical business during his four seasons as an Orangeman after having hit the mute button.

"I came in quietly," he said. "And I went out quietly."

And when Moten did, he took his 2,334 points—or 191 more than Coleman at No. 2—with him to professional gigs in the NBA, Spain, Venezuela, Greece and Puerto Rico. Moreover, he lugged away a seamless style that might not be observed anytime soon inside the Carrier Dome.

You see, the six-foot-five, 185-pound Lawrence Moten, who almost never breathed heavily and seemed rarely to sweat a drop, was a fascination. He had a push shot out of a grainy reel as opposed to a classic jumper, he always possessed more stealth than sinew, and he delighted in the idea that he was a kind of on-court sanitation engineer, cleaning up the messes made by others.

Efficient is what he was. Think of Ichiro, the baseball player, and you have Moten, the basketball player.

"The game is 90 percent mental and 10 percent physical," said Moten, who'd come to Syracuse out of New Hampton Prep School in New Hampshire. "My main thing was always to be an anticipator, to be in the right place at the right time. I've always been able to see things before they happen. It's called a knack. Some guys have it and some guys don't, and I've been blessed to have it. I just tried to blend everything I had together. You know, I tried to mix the old school with some of the new millennium stuff."

Well, it worked. Moten—who didn't bark or thump his chest or sneer at fallen foes—led Syracuse, almost silently, in scoring as a sophomore, junior and senior, and averaged 19.3 points per game during his Orange career that ended in 1995. And only three other SU players (who played more than one season) had a higher number than that—Bing (24.8), Smith (20.7) and Cohen (19.7).

Interestingly, it all began almost by accident on December 3, 1991—at the old ACC-Big East Challenge in Atlanta, Ga.—when Adrian Autry, one of Syracuse's guards, couldn't assume his position in the opening lineup because of a sprained ankle. This forced Jim Boeheim to tap his freshman, Moten, on the shoulder in the bowels of the Omni.

"I remember the exact moment when Coach Boeheim told me I'd be starting," Moten declared. "I remember being so happy that I went to the bathroom and out of the locker room and through the tunnel and under the arena to a telephone booth. And I called my mother. 'Mom,' I said, 'I'm starting.' And she said, 'Just do your thing, baby. Just do your thing.' So, I did."

He scored 18 points that night against Florida State as the Orangemen battered the Seminoles, 89-71. And a trend was begun because Lawrence Moten would start 117 of SU's next 118 games, 82 of which the Orangemen would win.

With, of course, his white socks yanked virtually all the way up to his knees.

"Where I'm from, people just naturally wear their socks high," said Moten, whose home has forever been Washington, D.C. "It's something I started doing in the fourth or fifth grade. People roll with it. I roll with it. If I don't have my socks up, it's like Superman without his cape."

So, what's to argue? Superman had his signature wardrobe, and saved Metropolis all those times...Lawrence Moten had his, and scored all those points. Same thing.

THE FOURTH (OR FIFTH)
OPTION MAKES GOOD

For a while there, Syracuse took its share of knocks for losing players via the transfer route. Never mind that so few of the expatriates carved out stellar careers with their new schools; it was chic to point fingers at the Orange program and whisper about the defections.

But something odd, and perhaps a bit unfair, developed during that time. Few mentioned Chuck Richards (from the U.S. Military Academy) and Leo Rautins (from Minnesota) and LeRon Ellis (from Kentucky) and Ryan Blackwell (from Illinois). That is, guys who transferred into SU rather than out of it, and thrived upon arrival.

Think about this: If it wasn't for one particular incoming transfer, it's possible that the Orangemen never would have marched onto the 1996 Final Four at The Meadowlands in New Jersey. That's right. If Jason Cipolla had jumped from Tallahassee Community College to Kentucky or DePaul or Florida or Florida State or Utah like he could have, Syracuse might not have survived those feisty Georgia Bulldogs in the West Regional in Denver, Colorado.

"Everyone knows that John Wallace hit the winning shot that night," Cipolla said. "He's famous for that, and he should be. But the way I look at it, if it wasn't for my shot, John never would have had the chance. We'd have been out of there."

Well, when a fella is right, he's right. The Bulldogs, after all, had erected a nine-point lead with fewer than three minutes to play and had possession of the ball. But the Orangemen clawed back, most notably behind a couple of three-point heaves by Lazarus Sims, to trail by two. And so, the game, the season and the Final Four dream were suddenly all on the same fragile line.

Enter Cipolla, the six-foot-seven junior from Queens, N.Y., with the accent that was as thick as a bus's exhaust.

"I was the fourth option," he remembered. "How does that sound? The play was basically set up for John to pass the ball in-bounds to Lazarus Sims, who was supposed to come off a screen and take the ball to the hole or get a good shot. Otis Hill was coming up the middle, John was stepping back in for a possible return pass and Todd Burgan was coming off something.

"Me? I guess I might have been the fifth option, the more I think about it. I started off at the foul line and just drifted and drifted and drifted...and John found me in the left corner. What'd we have left? Two-point-one seconds? In that situation, you have no time except to put the ball up. All my life, I'd never been shy about shooting. My motto always was: 'If you're not hot, get hot.' So, I shot it. And it went in, clean as a whistle. And as it did, I kind of fell back into the arms of Donovan McNabb, who was on the bench. Big Don. A good man."

The ball made the net dance as if a spring zephyr had passed through it. And just like that, the gripping affair was nudged into the extra session, where Wallace drained his legendary three-pointer just before the OT buzzer that allowed the prancing Orangemen to advance, 83-81.

The Georgia club, meanwhile, was devastated. And why wouldn't it be? The Bulldogs couldn't stop Wallace, who finished with 30 points and 15 rebounds, despite his sitting out 10 second-half minutes with foul trouble. And they realized it would be a long, long time before they'd forget the sight of the six-foot-eight forward dribbling the length of the floor and then canning that one final trey from the top of the key to break their hearts.

"Playing with John was a spectacular thing," said Cipolla, who'd finish his initial Orange campaign with a modest 7.7 scoring average—yet buried 17 points on that March evening in Denver. "He was flawless. He knew how to play the game. He was a very smart player who knew how and when to do things. He had great basketball intelligence, and you can't teach that."

And he had found the import from the Florida community college with the biggest pass of the storybook season.

"It was probably the greatest feeling I ever had," said Cipolla of the most extraordinary shot of his life. "It was a feeling that a lot of people will never have."

Just another transfer made good.

1996 FINAL FOUR:
THE ORANGEMEN PASS
ON THE ROMANCE

It had been seven years since the huzzahs had faded, which made for a fair amount of time for reflection and, perhaps, for a bit of softening. But Lazarus Sims, who bends as easily as a fence post, had little interest in either. Romance? As far as the Orangemen's 1996 run to the NCAA Tournament's championship game was concerned...well, you can put the romance out on the curb with the rest of the trash. Because that was all about truth merging with reality.

"We knew from the beginning of the season how good we were," said Sims, the senior point guard who'd choreographed SU's 29-9 season that included the school's third appearance in the Final Four. "We were around each other most of the summer and we knew each other from even before that. So, we had something there. Other people, outside our group, didn't recognize it. But it was there. We knew what we had. Nothing we did surprised us."

They were a funny bunch, those 1995-96 Orangemen. Their Final Four ancestors—the '75 gang that made it to San Diego and the '87 collection that ended up in New Orleans—were considered, in order, lovable rogues and spunky stars-in-the-making. And their descendants—the '03 troupe that returned to the Louisiana Superdome—were deemed the best thing to happen to Syracuse since the snow shovel.

But Final Four Edition No. 3—SU's '96 squad that drew its so-often icy inspiration from Sims and fellow senior, John Wallace—was different. Appreciated? Absolutely. Embraced? Sure. But different, if only because unlike those others, the Sims-Wallace Orangemen seemed to neither understand nor appreciate the very wonderment their gumption had inspired.

Never mind that Syracuse had entered the season on virtually nobody's top 25 list. Never mind that at no time between November and April did the team crack the top 10. Never mind that in the eight contests it played against clubs ranked among the nation's top six, it had lost six times.

Never mind that despite all of that, the Orangemen—undersized, slow afoot and only puddle deep—won 15 of their final 18 games and trailed heavily favored Kentucky in the title affair at the Meadowlands in New Jersey by just two points with fewer than five minutes to play. Seven years later, Sims still only shrugged.

"Kentucky wasn't too much for us," he insisted. "We should have won that game. We should have beaten them, and we all know it. It was just a couple of bad calls and a few situations that swung their way.

"But it was like that the whole tournament. Everybody figured we would lose every game we played. But from our standpoint, we didn't think anybody was better than us. Like Kansas in the West Regional. It wasn't us having to beat a great team. It was them having to beat us. And they didn't."

No, the Jayhawks of Paul Pierce and Raef LaFrentz and Scot Pollard and Jacque Vaughn did not. And in that NCAA tournament, neither did Montana State, nor Drexel nor Georgia nor Mississippi State.

And it was all so amazing. These Orangemen, remember, had been culled from local gyms. Jason Cipolla was from Queens, N.Y. Otis Hill was from White Plains, N.Y. Marius Januaryulis, the foreign kid, had gone to high school in Prattsburg, N.Y. Wallace was from Rochester, N.Y. Sims was from Syracuse. They, along with Todd Burgan and J.B. Reafsnyder—oh, and Donovan McNabb, the redshirt football quarterback who was leading the cheers from the bench—were it.

But it didn't much matter. Somehow, they found their way into the Final Four, where they inspired Rick Pitino's powerful Wildcats—Antoine Walker and Ron Mercer and Tony Delk and Walter McCarty and Derek Anderson and Mark Pope—to talk to God down the stretch.

"That's foolish to even think about," SU coach Jim Boeheim had admitted when he was asked if he'd considered picking the Orangemen to advance that far on the bracket sheet in his office pool. "That's fantasy to predict that."

But this particular fantasy did come through, thanks in large part to the miracle worked by the Orangemen against Georgia in the West Regional in Denver, Colorado. They were, after all, trailing by nine points with fewer than three minutes to play. And the Bulldogs had the ball. So, it was over. Done. Finished.

Except that it wasn't.

"At no time in that game did any of us figure we were out of it," said Sims, the six-foot-four kid from Henninger High who grew up to land a gig with the Harlem Globetrotters. "We believed we were going to the Final Four, regardless. It was a matter of doing what we needed to do and getting our part of the game going."

So, Sims—who took only 4.5 shots a game that year despite averaging 35.6 minutes of playing time—buried two three-pointers. And Cipolla splashed a jumper from the corner to force overtime. And Wallace won it, 83-81, with another three-pointer a blink ahead of the OT buzzer.

And just like that, the Orangemen had—as the old Baltimore Orioles manager, Earl Weaver, might have said— "Bela Lugosi-ed" the Bulldogs, and advanced. Ho and hum.

And, yeah, they actually smiled. Sims and Wallace, too. And for a moment, all of them were back in Hawaii, hooting and hollering with the wind in their hair.

"We were out there in December for the Rainbow Classic," Sims said, "and Coach Boeheim told us on the flight, 'No mopeds.' But we were just kids and we wanted to have some fun, so we snuck out and rented some. I think he saw us, though. Coach was sitting at a restaurant window and we went flying right past him. I mean, the whole team was in a pack, and we were going fast. Marius didn't know how to drive and he almost crashed. But Coach never said a thing."

Well, why would he? Boeheim's guys had just come off a 79-70 win over third-ranked Arizona in a stopover game en route to Honolulu. And the long campaign's winding road beckoned. And it promised to be bumpy.

"This was the first time in I-don't-know-how-many years that we hadn't been at least in the preseason Top 40," Boeheim would say three months later as his outfit prepared for another flight, this time to the Meadowlands. "But there was justification for it. It's always argumentative if you're 41st. You could be 31st. Or you could be 25th. But to get up to No. 4 (by virtue of a Final Four berth), that's a big jump."

Seven years later, Lazarus Sims—forever as romantic as a bag of bolts—still believed it was a jump the Orangemen should not have been asked to make. Hey, he's entitled.

DONOVAN MCNABB, SAVIOR

Before Carmelo Anthony sauntered along with his magnificent talent and winning smile, there was another Orangeman with pretty much the same blessed combination of ability and charm.

Once upon a time Donovan McNabb was Carmelo Anthony. Shorter, yes. A few pounds lighter, sure. And more famous for his spirals, absolutely. But McNabb lit up central and upstate New York in the mid and late 1990s just as Anthony would later do during the 2002-03 hoops season.

And while McNabb's stage was—first and foremost—the football field, he also had his moments on the basketball court. One, in particular.

First, though, a little history: Jim Boeheim, as most understand, looks upon schmaltz as if it was so much bad cheese on a refrigerator shelf. The long-time Syracuse coach isn't without imagination, mind you; it's just that he'd prefer all romance to steer clear of his basketball program. So when he was asked once too often about McNabb, who was no more and no less than another substitute off his bench...well, Boeheim hissed.

"Everybody," he said after the Orangemen had defeated Miami on February 1, 1996, "is writing about things that obviously have no meaning, and no importance, in the world at all."

So much for Boeheim's fascination with everybody else's fascination with McNabb, who was then a second-year freshman and only 80 months removed from signing a staggering $115-million contract with the NFL's Philadelphia Eagles.

Now, it wasn't that the coach didn't like McNabb, who'd ultimately depart SU as the school's greatest quarterback ever. Boeheim was, in fact, quite taken with the kid's athleticism and intelligence. It was just that Jim didn't have much use for a basketball player, any basketball player, whose football responsibilities prevented him from reporting to the gym before January. And that partially explains why McNabb played only 19 minutes—total—during his initial campaign that began for him a week or so after he'd led SU to a 41-0 victory over Clemson in the 1996 Gator Bowl and ended with him choreographing cheers from the Orange bench during the Final Four in the Meadowlands.

Ah, but then came the famous Georgetown game in McNabb's sophomore (and final) season with Boeheim's Orangemen. Then came the afternoon of February 8, 1997, inside the throbbing Carrier Dome where 29,877 roaring fans spilled from their seats. And the unimpressed coach became impressed.

SU won that day, toppling the Hoyas, 77-74, in a tong war featuring:

(1) A technical foul on John Thompson after the bellowing Georgetown coach had offered his spectacles to one of the game's on-court officials;

(2) A tangle between Syracuse's Jason Hart and the Hoyas' Victor Page; and

(3) A tussle involving the Orange's 212-pound Marius Januaryulis and Georgetown's 290-pound Jahidi White.

But make no mistake that SU would not have survived without the contributions of McNabb, the six-foot-three football headliner/basketball understudy who scored 10 points, grabbed six rebounds and blocked a shot in his 19 minutes off the bench. Why, even Boeheim noticed.

"It was a great game for him," the coach admitted. "He's a competitor. He's going to compete. He was, obviously, the difference in the second half."

McNabb? Shucks, he just sort of shrugged.

"This is something I've been doing since I was a kid," McNabb said...and it was true, as he'd been a hoops star (and Antoine Walker's teammate) at Mt. Carmel High School outside of Chicago. "I had an idea there were doubters out there. But I feel right now they'll tell me to keep working on basketball."

Maybe, but not all of them.

"When you start playing after football," said Boeheim, who can be stubborn, "I think it's going to take you a month to get ready."

"I don't think so," countered McNabb, who will be forever persistent. "It's all in the dedication and the athletic ability."

Not surprisingly, the coach's view ended up carrying much more weight. Not surprisingly, either, the player—who was given only 97 minutes spread across 13 games in that year of his unveiling against Georgetown—did not return for his junior or senior campaign.

"I talked to Donovan a few times about coming back," said Lazarus Sims, the SU point guard, six years after McNabb didn't. "And he told me, 'If Boeheim's not going to play me, why should I?' The funny thing is, Coach told Donovan if he would quit football and concentrate on basketball, he'd make him a starter or whatever. He was that good.

"Donovan was athletic. He could jump out of the gym. He could shoot. And because he had that football body, he was strong. It's just that he was better at football. But, wait. I don't know. Donovan probably could have been an NBA player. I'll bet he could still play today."

No doubt, he thinks about it. Especially when he and his Eagles are sweating through their helmets in summer camp beneath God's broiling sun.

"I love basketball," McNabb had said before leaving with only 18 games and a 2.3 scoring average on his two-season Syracuse resume. "In the fall, I'm a football player. In the spring, I'm a basketball player. And I know I can play both. I look to my future here and I see me playing basketball."

It never really did pan out that way, which may have been the Orangemen's loss. And Philadelphia's gain.

"I Don't Miss Games"

They've come in monstrous numbers, trudging through the wind and the rain and the snow and the sleet, to watch their Orangemen. And they've been doing so for years.

But while SU fans packed old Manley Field House to the point where fire marshals regularly descended upon the place for look-sees, the Orange faithful have been most famous for filling up the Carrier Dome, which they've been doing since the fall of 1980 when the concrete joint opened.

Why, in the building's first 23 seasons, including Syracuse's national championship campaign in 2002-03, 9,114,442 fans marched into the Dome for a total of 392 games, 328 of which the Orangemen won. That's a night-in-and-night-out average of 23,251, stretching from Danny Schayes to Carmelo Anthony...and that can be deemed some very serious staying power.

Among that bunch, of course, have been true zealots. And among those true zealots has been Bob Gilbert, who just might be the craziest of the crazy.

"I don't," he said, "miss games."

Hey, Mrs. Gilbert didn't raise a liar. And Bob Gilbert wasn't lying because from December 2, 1967, through March 9, 2003—a span of 35 years, 13 weeks and 6 days—he attended each and every one of the Orangemen's 555 home games.

Oh yes. Be advised that Bob lives just outside New Haven, Connecticut.

"It's a five-hour drive from my home to the Dome," Gilbert declared. "I don't push it. It's 300 miles, but it could be 296 or 294 depending on how many times I pass cars and switch lanes. I know to the minute when I'm going to arrive. Like, I'll call a friend from the road and say, 'When I get to town, let's go to dinner. I'll meet you at 17 seconds after 6:12 p.m.' And I'll pull up to the curb at 17 seconds after 6:12 p.m."

Now, you should know that Gilbert, who graduated from SU in 1971 and works for his family's glass business in New Haven, is nearly as devoted when it comes to road games, missing only a handful (i.e., the ones in Alaska and Hawaii) over the years. And, yeah, he's driven to the majority of those, as well, putting a total of more than 900,000 miles on three different Buicks, each of which was periodically steered through the kind of weather usually found just off the Bering Sea.

You're familiar with those lines "in sickness and in health" and "for richer or poorer" and "til death do us part," right? Turns out, they fit Bob Gilbert, who has been long wedded to SU basketball...and yes, that includes the "death" portion.

"I turned my car into a bomb," he confessed. "Remember the gas crisis when they were doing the odd/even thing with the license plates? I kind of pushed things back then.

"The Orangemen were playing down in North Carolina and I wasn't about to miss that one. Like I said, I don't miss games and I needed enough gas to get to and from North Carolina. So, I bought six-gallon and five-gallon and two-gallon and one-gallon gas cans, filled them up with gas and loaded the car with them.

"They were in the trunk. They were in the back seat. They were on the floor in the back. They were on the front seat next to me. They were on the floor underneath the glove box. That's why I bought all the different sizes. So they'd fit."

He got there, all right. He made it to and from North Carolina without blowing himself up and without getting arrested. And on that trip, Bob Gilbert not only watched his Orangemen, he acquired a skill.

"I put the Amoco gasoline in the front seat because I liked the smell of that gas better than the others," he said. "You know how some women can pick up the scent of perfume that other women are wearing? Well, I can tell one brand of gasoline from another. No, really."

The man was serious. Which goes a long way toward explaining why he's been single all these years.

"Nah, I'm not married," Bob said. "I'm still interviewing. But if I ever do get married, my wife is going to have to like going to basketball games."

HE CALLS 'EM LIKE HE SEES 'EM

By his reckoning, he's been an on-court visitor to the Carrier Dome at least once in every single basketball season played inside the joint since it opened in 1980. Which makes his a more familiar mug than that of even John Thompson, who stopped coming to Syracuse after walking away from the head of the Georgetown bench in 1999.

Tim Higgins, the famous game official, can probably walk into any saloon in town...and immediately get booed. And it doesn't bother him in the least.

"You see 'Syracuse' on the schedule and you wince, because you're going there for a night and you could get snowed in for a week," Higgins said. "Getting your rear end into that town and getting your rear end out of that town can be very difficult. That's why I don't mind when the people up there yell at me. I understand what's bothering them."

Yeah, yeah, yeah. The Orangemen play their games during the central New York winter, and there are times when the central New York winter can growl. And that can make travel something of a challenge. But in the case of Tim Higgins, what could possibly be the beef? After all, upon arrival he's had those Orangemen—so inquisitive, so chatty and with such angelic faces—waiting for him.

"I remember a game in the Dome when Pearl Washington was there," declared Higgins. "So, we're talking in front of Jim Boeheim right during the game. And Pearl asked as nice as you please, 'Do they have a referee school?' And I said, 'As a matter of fact, they do.' And then he asked, 'Did you go?' And I said, 'As a matter of fact, I did.' And then he sort of gave me this look and asked, 'Did you pass or fail?' Now, that was funny."

In hindsight, so were the developments at the end of a certain SU-Georgetown steel-cage match held in the Capital Centre in Washington, D.C.

"I forget the game," said Higgins, "but it was another one of those tough, intense, competitive things. Whatever, in the last 10 seconds, I make a call for Syracuse and Thompson starts rolling around in front of his bench, moaning and complaining. And Boeheim is telling me that only a great official with a lot of guts would make that kind of call, for the road team, that late in the game. I mean, he's giving me all the accolades an official can get.

"But with three seconds to play, I call a foul against Syracuse...and all of a sudden, Thompson is trying to embrace me and Boeheim is screaming that he's getting hosed by a home job. Boeheim had me going from the greatest referee in history to a bum in, like, seven seconds. And Thompson had me going the other way. And that's a true story."

As was this: When Higgins walked out of the building that March afternoon, the weather was more lamb than lion, a barometrical fact of D.C. life that allowed him to move on in his whistle-blowing world.

"Listen, the people in Syracuse are great," Higgins said. "The Dome is great. It's a fun, wholesome place. But I promise you that Syracuse has cost me more money than any other school in America because it can be so hard to get out of there and to the next game in the next town. I've been snowed in there a bunch, and it's a pain in the butt.

"Let's put it this way: If it was between a game in Syracuse and a game in Miami, I'd take the game in Miami 22 times before I'd take the game in Syracuse once. But that's nothing personal against the people there, because if they had their choice, they'd be with me in Miami. I like Syracuse. I really do. But I'd like it a lot better if it was 70 degrees outside."

So, what did you expect? He's Tim Higgins. He's the famous game official. The one who's blown his whistle in 10 different Final Fours. After visiting the Carrier Dome at least once every winter since 1980, he's just calling 'em like he sees 'em.

JASON HEART...ER, HART

Well, he is from Southern California. So what would you expect?

"When I think of Syracuse, I think of snow," said Jason Hart. "...In my freshman year, it snowed on Halloween and it didn't stop until April. I'm from Los Angeles, and on Halloween it's usually 75 degrees outside. So, I learned quick that snow was going to be my reality, and because I wasn't going home anytime soon, I had to get used to it. For me, it was, 'Welcome to a whole 'nother world.' Snow. That's what Syracuse is to me. Snow."

Pause. One...two...three...

"No, wait," Hart said. "Snow and the Carrier Dome. And if I could do it all over again, I would do it all over again."

Oh, once he settled in—once Jason Hart accepted his new address and stopped pondering a transfer to a school closer to his family out west—he came to love SU and his Orangemen. And why not? Hart, the six-foot-three guard who would leave the university as its all-time leader in steals and its No. 2 guy in total assists behind Sherman Douglas, was as competitive as any athlete ever imported by Jim Boeheim. And Syracuse did him the great favor of providing one of the college game's grandest pits of passion.

That's right—SU vs. Georgetown. Every year. Sometimes, even in the aftermath of the Big East Conference's hideous decision to expand and therefore dilute the schedule, twice.

"Each time we played, that game would get hyped on ESPN or CBS for days and days," recalled Hart, who was 5-1 against the Hoyas during his frigid stay. "And the players got hyped along with it. Finally, when we'd get to the locker room the day of the game, the music would be blaring. When we'd play them in the Dome, especially, it was big. Because we knew the fans would be there."

Well, sure. Between 1980-2003, the Dome had seen Orange basketball crowds of 30,000 or more a stunning 56 times...and on 14 of those occasions, the Hoyas provided the competition—including the afternoon of February 27, 2000, when 31,009 showed up to watch, among other things, Jason Hart play his final game in Syracuse.

"I always loved playing against Georgetown because of John Thompson," said Hart, referring to the Hoyas' hulking head coach. "It was like playing against a legend. He never spoke to the opponents, but he talked a lot to his players. He'd always be cussing at them, using all kinds of profanity. That's how he got their attention.

"With us, Coach Boeheim didn't swear that much. He had a different style. He'd always be screaming, but he didn't really use a lot of bad language. He just had that annoying voice of his. You know, it kind of sounded like, 'Yanh...yanh...yanh.' But I love Coach Bay. How can you not love him? He became a father when he was, like, 70 years old. Man, I wouldn't change a thing. If we didn't hear that voice, who knows? Everything might have been different."

And Jason Hart would have wanted none of that. He cherished his duels with Connecticut's Khalid El-Amin and Erick Barkley of St. John's and Pittsburgh's Vonteego Cummings. He enjoyed snorkeling, with Boeheim's blessing, with all of his teammates off the Hawaiian shore on the morning of the Maui Classic's championship game...and then beating Bobby Knight's Indiana Hoosiers for the title. He basked while leading his Orangemen to a No. 4 ranking down the stretch of his senior season.

But Hart really embraced those duels with Georgetown.

"I remember the first time we played them when I was a freshman," he said. "That was the year they had Victor Page and those guys. If you look at the tape, you'll see me arguing with Todd Burgan right near center court. There was a timeout, and we were going at it. I wanted to take the last shot as the shot-clock was winding down, and I was screaming for the ball. But Todd wouldn't pass it to me. I wanted to be 'The Man,' but he was already 'The Man.' It's kind of funny now when I think about it.

"And I remember the last time we played them. That was against Kevin Braswell and that bunch. It was a good game, like all the others. Everybody played hard. It wasn't like there was any hate or anything. I think things changed since the days of Derrick Coleman and Alonzo Mourning. I mean, it wasn't like there were elbows flying and stuff. But I remember it, mostly, because my parents were there to watch the last home game of my career. And that was nice."

Even with all that snow on the ground outside.

HE'S MR. FRENCH, WITH A STEEL GRIP

The Lone Ranger had Tonto, Johnny Carson had Ed McMahon, Batman had Robin. And Jim Boeheim has had Bernie Fine, his very own Mr. French, for more than a quarter-century...for nearly 1,000 games...for three glorious runs to the Final Four in three different decades. And the meter is still running on all of it.

Go on. Think about Orange basketball for these last 25 years or so. Do that, and Jim Boeheim's face quickly appears. But then, so too does that of Bernie Fine.

"Coach Fine is one of the finer points of Syracuse basketball," said Billy Celuck, the long-time backup center (and punster) out of suburban Scranton, Pennsylvania. "He knows more about the program, I think, than Coach Boeheim."

Maybe. Fine, after all, has been Boeheim's assistant—recruiting future stars, coaching the big men, salving egos, manning his clipboard—since Boeheim took the job in 1976. So, he knows every nook and cranny of the operation. And there is nothing to indicate that anything will change anytime soon. There will be Boeheim at the head of the SU bench for a good, long while...and there will be Fine (who, as Fred Lewis's team manager, met Boeheim in 1964) all but joined with him at the hip.

And that would be just peachy with the Orangemen, who've known a lifetime friend—and a character—when they've seen one.

"You look at him and you think he's just a fat dude," said Celuck, the seven-footer who played at Syracuse from 1998-99 through 2001-02. "But every day at practice, Coach Fine will tell you how he can set the meanest screens in the world. And then he does it. He'll stand out there with his little, pudgy body and then...boom. He'll knock you over like a big boulder."

Make no mistake that Bernie—who, when he chooses, can charm like a wire brush—is a tough one, all right. He is, after all, from Erasmus Hall High School in Brooklyn. And Brooklyn is no place for fine china.

"If you tick him off, he'll grab you by the neck bone and squeeze you," said Celuck. "He'll grab that muscle and bring you down to his size. He's known for that. He's got hands like steel. He's got the strongest grip I know of for an old man. Every day at practice, half of the guys would go running away from him because they knew what was coming. Coach Fine is the one who enforces the punishment, so when you're in trouble you avoid him."

And how many times did Celuck feel that infamous clamp on his skinny neck?

"Oh, wow," Billy responded. "I'd say about three times a week, every week, for five years. And I'm being serious."

The squeeze, apparently, has served Fine well. The squeeze, that is, in tandem with the man's knowledge. Because heading into the 2003-04 season, no other active Division I assistant coach had been at his post longer than Fine had been at his. That's staying power, folks. And along the way, Bernie had at least one big obstacle to overcome.

His wardrobe. Well, his trousers, anyway.

"I know about clothes," Celuck said. "My first day at school, I walked in the locker room wearing tight white pants and a tie-dyed shirt, and I had long hair and this big ol' head. And everybody started mocking me out and calling me 'Woodchuck.' Same thing with Coach Fine. We used to make fun of him, too.

"I mean, every day at practice he'd wear the same pants. Light blue felt warmup pants. I'm not kidding you. Every day, for five years. Ask any of the guys about Bernie Fine, and they'll tell you about his pants. Man, they were bad. But he was a good coach and a good guy. Anybody who ever played for him can pick up the phone any day or night and Coach Fine will be there."

Let's see. There is the grip. There are the pants. There are all those big men who've left SU as better centers and forwards than when they arrived. And there is the quarter-century and more of Orange loyalty. Put it all in the blender and mix it up...and Bernie Fine will spill out.

With clipboard in hand.

A WEEPER GREW IN BROOKLYN

There may be no crying in baseball, but basketball's a different story. Take Allen Griffin, the former Orange guard...but if you do, you'd better have some Kleenex at the ready.

"I cried after the last loss of every season I played," Griffin said. "We lost twice in the Sweet 16 and twice in the second round, and each time we did, I cried. I'm just being honest. What can I say? I'm emotional. I admit it. I cried.

"I was real close with Todd Burgan that first year when I was a freshman. And with Elvir Ovcina that second year when I was a sophomore. And with Jason Hart and Etan Thomas and Ryan Blackwell that third year when I was a junior. And then, when I was a senior, I was close to all the guys."

What happens is this: At the end of every college basketball season, developments always occur that break up the ol' gang. There are graduations and there are eligibility issues and there are transfers. And it all adds up to change. Nothing is ever the same from one campaign to the next, and the more passionate guys take it to heart.

Which is where Griffin—a six-foot-one kid out of Robeson High School in Brooklyn, N.Y.—comes in, because no Syracuse athlete could possibly have cared more for the precious present than he did while he suited up for SU between 1997-98 through 2000-01.

And that took some doing because Griffin's faith was sorely tested for a while there by Jim Boeheim. Allen did, after all, start every game as a sophomore and every game as a senior but none—zero, nada, zilch...not once in 32 contests—as a junior when he sat behind Tony Bland. And that felt like a thorn in a thumb.

"I was miserable," Griffin said. "In the end, it made me a better person and better prepared for life. I know that now. But at the time, I felt like my world was crashing. I had thoughts like, 'Does Coach Bay want me here anymore? Should I leave? Should I go to another school?' Really, I was miserable."

Well, of course. Griffin went from averaging 7.9 points and 3.2 assists in 27.2 minutes a game as a sophomore to 3.0 points and 1.7 assists in 10.7 minutes a game as a junior. So why wouldn't he suddenly feel as needed as a pair of suspenders at a nudist colony?

But Allen stuck it out, returned to the starting lineup as a senior and averaged 10.8 points and 6.5 assists in 36.7 minutes a game—and cried like a puppy in the dark when it was all over.

"It was the Kansas game in the NCAA Tournament," said Griffin of the Orangemen's 87-58 blowout at the hands of the bruising Jayhawks on March 18, 2001. "We were losing by a lot at the half, and then we cut it down and got back into it. But the next thing you know...well, let's just say they did a great job of beating us up.

"That was the team with [seven-foot Eric] Chenowith and [six-foot-10 Drew] Gooden and [six-foot-nine Nick] Collison. I mean, they were big. And all of a sudden it was over—the game, the season, my career, everything. And I knew that Coach Bay wasn't going to be my coach anymore. When I went to the bench with a couple of seconds to go, that's when the crying started. I had the big tears, and everything."

And when did he dry his eyes?

"Not," he answered, "for a week or two."

Oh, Griffin—who was bound for Greece in the summer of '03 for a shot at some European pro ball—took away some parting gifts. In his two seasons as a starter, for instance, the Orangemen went 46-21 and climbed on his senior watch to as high as No. 8 in the polls. He made a lifelong friend, specifically, with Mike Hopkins, the SU assistant with whom he worked for so many hours before and after practice. And he met his future bride, Tiffany Brown-Griffin, in a campus chow hall.

That last prize, though, has yielded some uncertain moments. Tiffany, you see, ended up being an adjunct professor at Syracuse with a Ph.D. in child and family studies. And that has led to some weighty conversations at the dinner table.

"I can't keep up with Tiffany all the time," Allen admitted. "I'll get halfway with her and then she completely loses me."

Sad, huh? Sad enough, almost, to make a grown man cry.

2003 Final Four:
Maybe It Was Won
Back in September

The greatest season in Syracuse basketball history began with a scene that had been often repeated some 40 years earlier when shorts were shorter, when hair was longer and when the Orange program was only beginning to stir anew.

Back then, the unsuspecting would enter Archbold Gym and encounter a sneakered magician who'd change their basketball lives. Yeah, Dave Bing had that kind of effect on people, who could do little more than look at the guy, shake their heads and look at him again. And then, after absorbing what they'd seen, they would consider the future and think only happy thoughts.

Well, history does have a way of repeating itself. And in September of 2002, it did.

"That first day, we were in Archbold Gym," recalled Kueth Duany, the captain and only scholarship senior on the SU team. "It was the first week of school and there were, maybe, eight of us there. Carmelo Anthony was one of them...and, to tell you the truth, it was hard to believe what I saw.

"It was his size. He was six-foot-eight, maybe 240 pounds because he wasn't in shape...but, man, did he move. I watched for a while and then I said to myself, 'This guy can't do this. He can't shoot threes like that. He can't handle the ball like that. He can't have agility like that. Not at that size.' But he did. He had all of it. He was bringing the ball up the court, dribbling between his legs, crossing guys over. I was, like, 'Man, he's legit. The hype is true. He's as good as they say. Maybe better.' I knew right then that we were going to be OK."

Maybe, but few others agreed. No preseason poll had SU in its Top 25. And Duany swore he remembered one list that had the Orangemen ranked 65th in all the land. Sixty-fifth! But then, who knew? Who really knew that Dave Bing had returned to Syracuse in the form of freshman Carmelo Anthony, an 18-year-old according to his birth certificate but a spectacle on the floor?

Now, it's true that the 2002-03 SU squad was more than just the smiley kid from Baltimore who rolled his hair into cornrows and then put a headband around the whole thing. Gerry McNamara and Billy Edelin, also freshmen, had stretches of dynamism. Hakim Warrick, Craig Forth and Josh Pace—all sophomores—were terrific when needed to be...sometimes subtly, sometimes not. Jeremy McNeil, a junior, morphed into a defensive colossus in the middle. And Duany, the dignified African-turned-American citizen, was the glue.

But it was Rick Barnes, the Texas coach, who said it best. Each point that the Orangemen scored, he insisted, could be traced to Anthony, whose mere presence forced six of the defenders' 10 eyes to be focused on him—the two of the poor soul assigned to guard him, and one each of the four who were guarding others.

"He is," insisted Jim Boeheim, the often-chilly coach who would be moved to later embrace Anthony and tell the kid that he loved him, "the best player in the country."

Who could argue? And why? Anthony would finish his freshman year with averages of 22.2 points and 10.0 rebounds. He would finish with 22 double-doubles. He would finish with a national championship crown on his head and the Final Four MVP award under his arm. And he would finish with the joy that comes with deliverance.

"I brung Coach Boeheim what he was waiting for for 27 years," Anthony said (in his best Dizzy Dean) when it was all over. "I brung a lot out of the community, as well as Syracuse University. I think I brung the community back and put them where they wanted to be. They've been waiting for this for a long time. I gave them what they wanted."

It began in Boston, Massachusetts, SU's NCAA Tournament run did, with a breezy win over Manhattan (76-65), followed by a staggering comeback from a 17-point deficit and a subsequent knockout of Oklahoma State (68-56). And it continued the following weekend just down the Thruway in Albany, N.Y., where the Orangemen survived Auburn (79-78) before burying Oklahoma (63-47).

And that landed Syracuse in the Final Four in New Orleans where 16 years earlier Keith Smart turned out the lights all across central and upstate New York by hitting the jumper that ended the magnificent Orange dream of a national championship.

The Hoosiers, though, weren't around this time; instead, yet two more clubs from the Big 12 Conference, Texas and Kansas, were waiting. And the masses—108,956 over the two steamy nights—came out for a look-see.

"Texas' whole game was transition," said Duany of Saturday's semifinal that was won by SU, 95-84. "They wanted to push the ball against us. It was one of those things where, 'As T.J. Ford goes, so goes Texas.' So, our whole focus was to cut the head off the dragon. And we did because Ford had a tough game, a tough night."

The spectacular Anthony, meanwhile, scored 33 points and hauled in 14 rebounds. And McNamara (19), Warrick (18) and Pace (12) combined for 49 points, plus 13 rebounds and 10 assists. Which meant the Longhorns were heading home and giving way to the Jayhawks. To the very, very good Jayhawks.

"You know how everybody fills out a bracket before the Tournament begins?" Duany said. "Well, Kansas was the team I was worried about. I remember when we played them in the Tournament when I was a sophomore. I mean, they hammered us (87-58). I think they outrebounded us by about 50. It was like we didn't belong on the same court with them. So, I reminded the guys that we had to pay them back."

They did, as McNamara was a first-half sensation with 18 points on six-of-eight shooting from beyond the arc and Anthony was a picture of steady brilliance with his 20 points, 10 rebounds and seven assists. But the Orangemen may have survived because the basketball gods have long memories and they'd determined Syracuse had been haunted enough by the vision of the Smart shot that never did get blocked.

And so, those gods sprung Warrick on KU's Michael Lee, who went up with the jumper that, if drained, would have sent the mad affair into overtime.

"You know, we'd probably seen the Keith Smart shot 1,000 times," Warrick said. "So, when Lee went up for the shot, I was, like, 'Oh, no.' I just didn't want that happening to Coach Boeheim again."

"The guy was completely wide open," said Duany. "So, I started sprinting towards him and as I was, he was getting his shot off. I just figured he was going to make it. I mean, he's not going to miss that shot. He's just not. And then, out of the corner of my eye, I saw Hakim come flying by. I mean, he was flying, man. Flying."

And he reached Lee just in time, batting the ball into the seats with two seconds to play, hence preserving the most wondrous victory in the history of Syracuse basketball, 81-78.

"Awesome," Duany said. "It was awesome then. And it's awesome now, remembering it."

Just that quickly, Hakim Warrick had become another in the long line of SU legends. And because he did, tears of joy moistened cheeks down in the bayou, for sure, and also across the breadth of the Orange Basketball Nation that had been established back in 1901.

"The euphoria?" said Duany. "Oh, man, it was even greater than I thought it ever could be. I mean, it's hard to describe how it felt. Are you kidding? Just talking about it now, three months later, I'm getting the sweats."

And why not? Kueth Duany had been there when it began. Better yet, he'd recognized the greatness back then in September. He was in Archbold Gym, after all, when Carmelo Anthony walked into it for the first time some 40 years after Dave Bing had done exactly same thing. And just like that, Duany's mind filled with happy thoughts.

ROY DANFORTH BETS ON A SURE THING

Joe Louis, the great boxing champion, used to say, "If you've got to tell them who you are, you ain't." Which is why, in those years after he left the ring, he chose to stand in line for a restaurant table like everybody else.

It is partially for that reason that Louis would likely enjoy the company of Roy Danforth, who believes he's as important as a spare button.

"I've won more drinks in more gin mills than I can remember," Danforth announced. "I'll be at the bar and the Syracuse game will come on TV, and I'll bet the yokels sitting next to me a beer. 'Who coached the Orangemen before Jim Boeheim?' And nobody ever knows. Then, I say, 'Roy Danforth,' and everyone pays up."

Interestingly, he never follows that answer with the words, "And I'm Roy Danforth." Even as he's heading for the parking lot.

"Nah," said Danforth, who is living in retirement on Cape Cod. "I don't identify myself. That's not the kind of guy I am. I've got a couple of bars I go to around here, I have a few drinks and then I go home. And nobody knows who I am. When the Final Four came around, the local newspaper guy never called. Syracuse called. New Orleans called. But not the local guy. Nobody has any idea who I am, and I like that."

Go figure, huh? The man who led SU to its first Final Four berth in 1975 (and turned that San Diego affair into his own Comedy Club)...the man who guided the Orangemen to a 148-71 record in his eight seasons as head coach...the man who possessed enough foresight to hire Jim Boeheim as a graduate assistant in 1969...the man who did all of that is content these days to read, play bridge and sail his boat, Benediction, in anonymity?

"I like my privacy," Danforth said. "That's why I live here."

Oh, the old U.S. Army paratrooper is still a pip when you get him on the telephone. He can still break eggs as if it's '75 all over again and Seibert and Kindel and King and DeMarle and Parker are trolling about the floor of the San Diego Sports Arena with their bad hair and/or bad bodies. And he knows it.

"I say, if you can't afford to go out, stay home," Danforth declared. "I'm a happy-go-lucky, fun-loving sailor. If you can't take a joke, the hell with ya."

As such, he remembers Boeheim, who grew up to choreograph Syracuse's 2002-03 national championship season, in his own way.

"He has great basketball knowledge," Danforth said. "There's no question about it. But Freddie Lewis used to think Jimmy was a pain in the butt because he always had an opinion. And Boeheim was never wrong in his own eyes. Me? He used to get ticked at me all the time because I harassed him about not going into the Army. 'If you were a man,' I'd tell him, 'you'd enlist and do your time.' He didn't like that."

He was a different bird, Danforth was. Colorful threads. Slicked hair. Fast mouth. And an intriguing background. He'd grown up in Indiana, played basketball at Southern Mississippi, jumped out of 32 perfectly good airplanes while serving three years in the Army, and coached at Pearl River Junior College in Poplarville, Mississippi, before Lewis, SU's head man, rescued him in 1964. And upon arrival in Syracuse at the age of 28, he had his eyes opened after engaging in three-on-threes with Boeheim and Dave Bing and the boys.

"I was just a country boy and I was kind of full of myself," said Danforth, who was Lewis's one and only assistant but had a job load that also included teaching P.E. classes, coaching the freshman team, recruiting and scouting. "But I had never seen players that good before. I was amazed. I had no idea that Syracuse was such a good basketball program."

It wasn't good enough, though, to prevent Lewis—who'd grown tired of feeding off football's scraps—from fleeing to Sacramento State in 1968 and flipping the keys to Danforth as he walked out the door. The Orangemen's response? They lost their first five games under the new guy, won only 21 of their initial 49...and then, with some help for a while from "Roy's Runts," went to two NITs and four NCAA tournaments in six consecutive campaigns.

And, yeah, that encompassed the glorious 1975 run to Southern California where the tall Final Four cotton—too tall, as it turned out—of UCLA, Kentucky and Louisville awaited.

"I love Syracuse, I really do," Danforth said. "And if you love Syracuse, you can love anything. I lived there for 13 years and saw the sun three times. You're always freezing your butt off in Syracuse. You're always up to your butt in snow in Syracuse. And I knew the guys knew this. So about halfway through that season, before every game I'd write on the corner of the blackboard, 'It's nice in San Diego at this time of year.' That became our motto. Well, we got there. We didn't win, and maybe we were lucky along the way, but we got there."

It wasn't enough, however, to inspire Danforth to embrace the Syracuse weather he loathed because he left to coach at Tulane in 1976 and then moved on to Fairleigh Dickinson for a while to become its athletic director before settling down in Osterville on the Cape where, Danforth insists, "I have exactly two distinctions: (1) I'm the only Democrat living here, and (2) I'm the poorest guy in town."

There is, of course, a third distinction. Roy Danforth is the only resident of Osterville to have coached a team to the Final Four. Not that anybody in the local gin mills knows.

BLESSED ARE THE LITTLE GUYS

It was Wilt Chamberlain, the seven-foot-one basketball leviathan, who once lamented that nobody loved Goliath. And he was right. We stand agog in the presence of size and strength, but we want to take the little guys home for dinner.

And, in regard to Syracuse hoops history, it has been no different during the Jim Boeheim era, which began in 1976 and, 879 games later, produced a national championship.

Go on. List your favorite Orangemen in all that time...you know, along with Carmelo Anthony. Do that, and far, far sooner than later three names will likely pop up.

Dwayne Washington. Sherman Douglas. Gerry McNamara.

The Pearl. The General. G-Mac.

And not one of them ever saw beyond six-foot-two.

In terms of impact, of course, it could be stated that Washington—joined by Dave Bing and Anthony—is a member of SU's holy basketball trinity. More than his career per-game averages of 15.7 points and 6.7 assists, it was his combination of chutzpah and charisma that so endeared Washington to Syracuse fans and made the Carrier Dome *the* place to be on a cold winter night.

And all these years later—Washington did leave the Orangemen for the NBA, after all, in 1986—he remains revered.

"It's nice to know that people still appreciate you," said the six-foot-two Pearl, whose 40th birthday will be celebrated in January of 2004. "When I'm out, they come up to me all the time and say, 'Thank you.' They're not crazy about it; they just want me to know they haven't forgotten me or what I did here. Believe me, I hear it every day. Every day."

The compliments come with ease to Washington, who lives in town and works for the Syracuse Parks and Recreation Department. But Douglas—who dressed for the Orangemen between 1985-86 through 1988-89—is forced, mostly, to rely on his memories.

After playing 12 NBA seasons for five different franchises, Sherman—who is sneaking up on 40, himself—has long since moved away. But his ears still ring from that March night in 1989 when he became SU's all-time leading scorer (on a breakaway dunk, of all things) and the NCAA's career assists leader—both in a span of two minutes and 44 seconds.

And, yeah, the Dome—stuffed with 29,124 roarers—went up for grabs. Twice.

"I think," Douglas would later say in a quiet locker room, "that was the loudest I've heard the fans cheer here."

Well, of course. He was the new Pearl, only two inches shorter. And to embrace Washington was to embrace Douglas, who departed SU with career per-game averages of 14.9 points and 7.0 assists.

"'Inventive' is the word for him," said Connecticut coach Jim Calhoun, whose Huskies were Sherman's foils that enchanting evening. "Some of those things he does, I've never seen before. And we probably won't again."

Those words made sense then, but 14 seasons later, we caught another glimpse of Douglas—and, therefore, of Washington—in the person of McNamara, the stunning six-foot freshman from Scranton, Pennsylvania, who averaged 13.3 points and 4.4 assists for a championship club. McNamara made everybody stop and point and smile at the little guy all over again. Including, even, his teammates.

"Gerry awed me almost every time he did his stuff," said Kueth Duany, the senior captain who was speaking for so many. "He's a hard hat. Once the whistle blows for the tipoff, the guy is fearless. He doesn't back down from anybody. He makes plays, man. He's got guts. Huge, huge guts. And he makes plays."

It is a one-size-fits-all description of the three of them, isn't it? None stood taller than six-foot-two. None will ever have to duck when passing beneath the Mistletoe. None has yet to be asked to lower his head at the movies. Each, though, is as big as big gets in Orange hearts.

The Pearl. The General. G-Mac. Little guys...beloved guys...the non-Goliaths of a storied program. And each makes everybody's short list of favorite Orangemen far, far sooner than later.

THE SMILE

There are smiles out there. Signature smiles. Legendary smiles. We-wouldn't-know-them-any-other-way smiles. Julia Roberts has a smile. Robert Redford has a smile. Heck, the Mona Lisa has a smile...sort of.

It's been said that smiles can make the rain stop, which means that the folks of Syracuse, who too often stroll beneath weepy skies, are always looking for some good ones. And that helps to explain, in part, the attraction of Carmelo Anthony in central and upstate New York.

The 18-year-old kid played only one season for the Orangemen—the magical 2002-03 campaign during which he delivered a national championship—before leaving for the riches of the NBA. And during that one season he scored (22.2 points per game) and rebounded (10.0 boards per game) and passed (2.2 assists per game).

But, importantly, Anthony did it with a stunning effervescence. With obvious delight. With a smile so bright, it could lead miners out of a cave-in. And that begs the question: From where did that smile come?

"I can trace it back to when he was two years old," said somebody who should know—Carmelo's mother, Mary Anthony. "Carmelo would go out on the playground, have fun and come home with this great, big smile. He loved to play with the kids. The way you see him now, with that great, big smile? That's the way he's been since he was two."

Now, it should be known that Carmelo was something of a coddled child. He was raised in a tough Baltimore neighborhood dubbed "The Pharmacy" because of the volume of illicit drugs bought and sold and used up and down the hard streets that swallowed so many of his neighbors as if they were after-dinner mints. But despite the frightening environment, Carmelo was not only loved and protected, but favored.

"Truth is, he was spoiled," said Mary. "Still is. Everybody has spoiled Carmelo going back to when he was a baby. His brothers, his sister, his uncle...everybody. But he's always been a special child, a loving kid. He was a fun baby. From the time he was two years old, he was exciting to be around. Everyone loved just being with him. Because he was always smiling."

Certainly, SU's legions of fans understand because they saw it for themselves. They saw Anthony smile when he missed free throws...they saw Anthony smile when the patrons in opposing arenas ribbed him from the stands...they saw Anthony smile when he applied a friendly in-game shoulder rub to an enraged Mike Jarvis, the St. John's coach who was at the time jawing with a referee along a Carrier Dome sideline. And so on and so forth.

Make no mistake that Carmelo Anthony, the fabulous freshman, was so very popular during his one year in town because he was majestically talented (and the Orangemen went 30-5). But a fool is that person who would underestimate the powerful effect Anthony's personality had on the community. And in the Syracuse locker room, too.

Ask Mary and she'll reveal the "dark" side of Carmelo. The youngest of her four children, she'll confess, won't eat his vegetables, refuses to clean his room and doesn't much care for cats and dogs. But he does smile, and when he does, all that other stuff goes away.

"He takes me back to the days of Julius Erving," Mary said. "I see my son as Julius Erving. No matter how tough the game was going, Julius had that smile. When I see Magic Johnson, I see my son. Magic just takes over the crowd. Everybody he meets is drawn to him. That's Carmelo. There's something about his look, his expression, his smile that draws people. People talk to Carmelo and they end up laughing."

OK, fine. But again, from where did it come?

"I'm a joyful kind of person," Mary said. "I think he got it from me."

And then, Carmelo Anthony's mom smiled. Naturally.

PEREZ CELIS SLAM DUNKS...
WITH A BRUSH

As the 2002-03 Syracuse basketball team marched to the national championship, its bandwagon steadily grew to the size of a barge, and so filled was the thing with fans that it seemed sure to sink to the bottom of the Orange River.

Ultimately, the SU faithful would spread from Bangor to Bakersfield, from Sarasota to Seattle, from Fargo to Fort Worth. Nobody, but nobody, seemed to be able to get enough of Carmelo Anthony and his merry teammates. And as the clamor grew, it appeared that everyone wanted to share the joy.

Turns out, the fever seeped even into the soul of a celebrated Argentine artist named Perez Celis, a native of Buenos Aires who was so taken with all things Orange that soon after the final horn at the Louisiana Superdome he was compelled to grab his brush and get busy on a canvas. The result was a five-foot-by-four-foot commemorative painting of Anthony and Jim Boeheim titled, "It Is More Than Just Trying To Get The Ball In The Basket."

"All I remember of the games I saw in Syracuse," Celis said, "is the passionate, colorful comings and goings of very driven young men."

Now, what you absolutely need to know about Perez Celis is this: As his pieces have been displayed in the Museum of Modern Art in New York City and in the Library of Congress in Washington, D.C., he is as blessed around his easel as Gerry McNamara is at the foul line.

You also need to know that Celis, an ardent soccer follower and, annually, a visiting artist in various classes on the SU campus since the last stand of Etan Thomas and Jason

Hart, has also become Argentina's foremost Syracuse basketball nut.

"This is a one-of-a-kind situation," Celis said after the Orangemen had knocked off both Texas and Kansas at the Final Four. "And I want to give something special to Syracuse, which has been so nice to me. I can do better than a poster. Let's see, lately I was thinking [about] something new in terms of color."

With that, the 58-year-old Celis went to work—sometimes beginning at 5 a.m., sometimes ending at 1 a.m.—and the result was a splash of orange and red and green and yellow and purple/pink. Do you recall those scenes in *Field Of Dreams* during which the characters disappear into the stalks of corn? Well, Celis went the other way. He made Anthony and Boeheim magically emerge from his mix of fanciful colors.

And his presentation to the university gave the SU fan who had everything—shirts, caps, mugs and so on and so forth—an eye-popping option. Indeed, soon after its completion in April of 2003, Celis's painting was thoughtfully turned into a full-color poster, priced at $25, the proceeds of which will be funneled into the Jim Boeheim Scholarship Fund.

Which means this: You can now have a Celis on your wall, which is only fair. Because chances are, Celis has a Syracuse pennant on his.

(Those interested in purchasing a full-color copy of Perez Celis's "It Is More Than Just Trying To Get The Ball In The Basket" can obtain information from Syracuse University's Point of Contact at 315-443-2247.)

DEAN AND THE BARON
MAY HAVE COMPANY

Reggie Jackson, the baseball star, once likened a lifetime's pursuit of statistics to heading into a bountiful orchard with an empty basket. The idea, he insisted, was to avoid too much talk and simply go about filling the basket.

OK, so Reggie didn't avoid talking. But if you'll accept his imagery, you can't help but come to the conclusion that Jim Boeheim has plucked an awful lot of apples during his time as the head basketball coach of the Orangemen.

"How," asked his former player and assistant, Louis Orr, "can anyone even think about winning as many games as Jim Boeheim has won?"

After walking out of the Louisiana Superdome with the 2003 national title tucked under his arm, Boeheim's record stood at 653-226, which computed to an average season of 24-8 scattered across 27 Syracuse campaigns.

More remarkable yet, the pride of Lyons, N.Y., has been at SU and involved in some capacity with the Orange program—as a player, part-time coach, graduate assistant, aide or head man—pretty much without interruption since 1962. And during that time, from '62-'03, Syracuse had played 1,246 of its 2,351 games.

Which means, simply, that the fingerprints of one man can be found on 53 percent of all of SU's games waged since 1901. One man. Jim Boeheim. No wonder, then, that the university named its basketball court after him in 2002. And no wonder, too, that Jason Hart, who closed out the 20th century as SU's feisty four-year starter at point guard, maintains that "Coach Boeheim is a legend, a living legend, and now that he's won his championship, everybody in the world knows it."

"I cannot even begin to comprehend Jim Boeheim's longevity," said Orr, the one-time Orangeman and current head coach at Seton Hall. "I don't know how anybody could ever imagine doing what that man has done."

Hey, give Boeheim 10 more years at his current pace and he blows by both Dean Smith (879) and Adolph Rupp (876), who sit 1-2 at the top of the leaderboard in all-time Division I coaching wins. Give him an 11th year, and he clears the 900 barrier. Give him 15, and he vaults 1,000. Gulp.

Amazing...particularly when one considers Boeheim's early forecast.

"I remember after a couple of years," he said, "I was telling people I'd never make five."

Well, Boeheim has made it past the quarter-century pole and, with his 2003 title, became one of just 39 coaches—divvied up among only 29 schools—to win a national title since the inception of the NCAA Tournament in 1939. And he's done it with intelligence and tenacity, sure, but also with an ability to appeal to players.

And that allure mattered to Boeheim's first big recruit, Roosevelt Bouie, back in the mid-'70s.

"When I was a kid, I used to go to the Syracuse camp in the summer," said Bouie. "I remember I saw Coach Boeheim come back from golfing one day, and he had on a pair of plaid shorts and a T-shirt and some low-cut Converse sneakers...and he didn't really have his feet in them all the way. You know, he was kind of walking out of the back of the things. I looked at him and I thought, 'Man, he's just a relaxed guy.' That was the kind of feeling I wanted to have with my head coach."

So, Bouie signed on with the Orangemen. And through the years, so did Orr and Leo Rautins and Danny Schayes and Rafael Addison and Dwayne Washington and Rony Seikaly and Derrick Coleman and Sherman Douglas and Stephen Thompson and Billy Owens and LeRon Ellis and Dave Johnson and John Wallace and Lawrence Moten and Etan Thomas and Jason Hart and Damone Brown and Carmelo Anthony—each of the 18, an NBA player—and so many others, too.

Hey, they saw what was happening in Syracuse. They saw a man out in the orchard picking all those apples, and they wanted a clear look inside his basket.

J2: THE RETURN OF JIMMY BOEHEIM?

The day was April 24, 2003. The Syracuse University basketball team had won the national championship only 17 days earlier, central and upstate New York were still basking in the glow of that title, flowers bloomed in every garden. Life, in other words, was just dandy in Orange Nation.

But then word got out: SU was calling the 2 p.m. news conference that nearly everybody had hoped would never be convened. Surely, Carmelo Anthony, the magnificent freshman forward, was going to declare his intention to leave school and sign on with the NBA.

And so, the news gatherers—scores of them—descended upon Manley Field House, which was to serve as the site of the melancholy affair. And they pointed their cameras and microphones and notepads in the direction of an empty table and three empty chairs. And they waited.

Finally, Jim Boeheim, the 58-year-old Syracuse coach presented himself, cleared his throat and started to say the words that all witnesses believed they didn't want to hear.

"I think," he announced to the breathless room, "there is an outside chance that Jimmy Boeheim might commit today to come to Syracuse. But I've got to check with his mom first."

There was laughter. There was hope. After all, there was no Carmelo Anthony in sight, but there was little Jimmy Boeheim, the coach's young son, squirming on the lap of his mother, Juli Boeheim, near a far wall.

Hey, maybe, just maybe, Carmelo wasn't leaving. Maybe, just maybe, this was all a friendly joke.

But, no. Anthony, the great Anthony, walked through the door just then and said good-bye through a cracked voice and with teary eyes. And the joke was no more.

DIRECT FROM THE E-MAIL BAG

On the evening of April 7, 2003, thousands of Syracuse University basketball fans marched upon the Carrier Dome to gaze at three huge television screens and watch the Orangemen play the Kansas Jayhawks in the national championship game.

That affair was taking place in another vast building, the Louisiana Superdome, down in New Orleans where still thousands of other SU pilgrims had gathered to roar into the bayou night. But those folks up in Syracuse, the ones who'd converged for the communal experience of their lives, might just as well have been in New Orleans. Such was their passion.

One of those in the crowd was Lou Cinquino, a true Orange zealot (and, evidently, a learned Orange historian) who drove in from his home in Emmaus, Pennsylvania, to share the moment with two friends. So inspired by SU's ultimate 81-78 triumph was Cinquino, who graduated from Syracuse in 1984, that he felt compelled to send an e-mail to a columnist at *The Post-Standard* newspaper.

Writing, certainly, for most folks throughout central New York, these were some of the words Lou tapped out on his computer...

"I need some sleep. I've been up all night, so forgive me if this doesn't all make perfect sense. But here it is. Here's what it felt like to be on the other side of one of these things. The winning side.

"The far end zone of the House That Pearl Built was orange from head to toe and filled with undergrads who confidently expected nothing short of victory. And why not? They weren't even old enough to read back then when SU last went to New Orleans with a brash, athletic team that reached the Final Four's championship game only to be done in by Keith Smart.

"But the Carrier Dome was also filled with older, more experienced people who knew the meaning of proudly wearing one's heart on one's sleeve. We needed those naive kids to help us forget about that loss to Smart and Indiana...and they needed us to make the night as much about redemption as a reason to party.

"The Dome went quiet for long, painful stretches in the second half when Kansas made its runs, largely because those young kids didn't really understand the ebb and flow of the high-wire act called Syracuse basketball. But those who'd been there before with the Orangemen—that is, the elders in the place—recognized what was unfolding. As such, we tried our best to fight off the temptation to replay every previous collapse and every previous storied victimization that we had endured.

"We were sure that we were once again watching Derrick Coleman miss a one-and-one in the final minute...Howard Triche's feet moving not nearly fast enough...Lawrence Moten's ill-advised timeout...No. 15 Richmond's disregard for our No. 2 seeding...Walter Berry's last stand...Rick Pitino's first NBA team (i.e., that Kentucky outfit which showed up for the title affair in 1996)...and others that escape clarity but are woven into the very way we watch a game.

"But then, every Syracuse basket down there in the Superdome was celebrated as if man had landed on the moon for the first time (did we ever expect to live to see this day?). Every Kansas miss boosted our self-esteem (poor bastards, we know something about clanked free throws). Every monster rebound by some Orangeman or another was saluted (or at least all those rebounds that Nick Collison didn't grab, himself).

"And the memories suddenly came to life to play tricks in ways none of us ever could have imagined.

"Was that Coleman tipping away the Jayhawks' free throws? Was that Triche jumping three feet into the air to block that last shot from the corner? Was that Moten ticking off the final seconds of the clock rather than trying to stop it?

"Funny, but suddenly it was Gerry McNamara and not Steve Alford or Tony Delk having a career night from three-point range. It was our NBA-bound hero, Carmelo Anthony, willing his team to victory and not all of those NBA-bound Wildcats and their NBA-bound coach. In short, it was all so very different.

"And then...well, then the bizarre parallel universe really manifested itself because there was Jim Boeheim telling Roy Williams what Bobby Knight had whispered 16 years earlier. 'You'll be back,' Jimmy told the Kansas coach.

"Yes, the Orangemen had won. And, of course, a party ensued and we tried to make sense of what had just been witnessed up there on the big screens inside the Carrier Dome. And when we'd finished reconstructing the game, and in particular its final moments, and determining that what we'd just seen actually did happen, my two friends and I ventured into the early morning in search of something to eat.

"After a long, meandering, icy and seemingly fruitless drive, we came upon a place that made good on its promise of breakfast, complete with three searing cups of joe. It was there, in the deepest part of the night and in the very heart of the city, that we enjoyed the last of our one shining moment.

"At some point, just as the sun was gathering itself to rise for the first time on Championship City, we began to head back home. But before we did, we needed to gather some evidence to prove that everything had, in fact, happened as we thought it did. We needed to know that the Orangemen had defeated the Jayhawks and that they really were the national champions.

"So, we bought some newspapers and read all about it."

Epilogue

They'd survived the last, late push by Kansas down there at the Louisiana Superdome in New Orleans. The Orangemen had built the big lead, stood up to the Jayhawks' waves like a great seawall and watched with near-awe as one of their own, Hakim Warrick, soared through the air to block the shot just before the final buzzer that preserved the dream.

And, with the 81-78 victory assured, the 2003 national championship was theirs.

The noise, of course, was thunderous. And the tears of all those old Orangemen who'd come down to the bayou to take in some history flowed. And joyful chaos reigned.

Jim Boeheim? He was spent. So spent, in fact, that he wanted to flee the building even before CBS fired up its annual "One Shining Moment" ode to the victors.

"I was tired," the 58-year-old coach explained. "I get tired at these games. I don't have the stamina I used to have. I was ready to go."

They'd been playing basketball at his school since 1901. He'd suited up there in the 1960s, teaming his entire career with the wondrous Dave Bing. He'd served as assistant or head coach during SU's three previous (and fruitless) visits to the Final Four. And now, in the midst of the happy din, Jim Boeheim's wish was to sneak out a side door?

What could possibly have been on the man's mind?

"Actually, right about that time," he said, "I was thinking about what we were going to do next year."

A coach. Always a coach.